Beginning Psychology

Beginning Psychology

Malcolm Hardy
Steve Heyes

Lecturers in Psychology,
South Trafford College of Further Education

Weidenfeld and Nicolson
London

*To Pam, Trish, Emma, Agnes, Sam, Eileen, Len and Tim,
and to our students – past, present and future.*

Weidenfeld and Nicolson
91 Clapham High Street   London SW4

ISBN 0 297 77594 4 cased
ISBN 0 297 77595 2 paperback

Printed in Great Britain by
Butler & Tanner Ltd
Frome and London

Contents

Preface

At a party given by an astronaut and his wife it was discovered that the household's electric kettle had broken. The woman asked each guest in turn to mend it (they were all expert engineers). None of them would attempt it, and all gave the same reply: 'Sorry, ma'am, I'm not that kind of engineer.'

Often the response of people who are asked to take part in a psychology experiment is, 'What will it tell me about my personality?' even when it has been explained to them that the experiment is designed to measure something as unromantic as speed of reaction. Psychology is becoming more and more specialized. Few psychologists spend their time sitting next to patients lying on couches; these days a psychologist is likely to be an expert in a particular field – learning, memory, or perception, for example – and not in psychology as a whole: 'Sorry, ma'am, I'm not that kind of psychologist.' However, psychologists have one thing in common: they all study *behaviour*. Behaviour is a very broad term; anything an organism, whether human or not, does, is behaviour. This explains why nobody is an expert in psychology as a whole: there is simply too much behaviour for one person to understand.

The aim of this book is to show how different psychologists approach the study of behaviour, and to describe the kinds of things which they have found. No book could hope to show all the findings gained over the last ninety years or so in which scientific psychology has largely developed. We have therefore aimed to provide a linking theme throughout the book: 'How does the individual develop throughout life?'

The first two chapters could well be subtitled 'The nuts and bolts of behaviour'. They deal with physiologists' and psychologists' findings about the ways in which the nervous system works, and its influence on our behaviour. Chapter 3 examines how the genetic blueprints for the body are passed on from parents. Chapters 4 to 7 examine how we develop the abilities to receive, store and use information; and chapters 7 and 8 examine some of the complex ways in which the genetic blueprint can be altered by the environment during the development of behaviour. Chapters 9, 10 and 11 investigate what psychologists have found out about the factors affecting development of the individual's social behaviour, and chapter 12 describes a field of study which is becoming very popular – the ways other than language in which we communicate. Chapter 13 looks at some of the major factors which seem to lead to conformist behaviour. The final two chapters examine how the individual continues to develop in adulthood and old age, and suggest some of the major influences on our behaviour at work, and the effects of ageing on development.

We have introduced the theme of the progress of the individual from conception to death as a way of connecting the findings from several different areas of psychological research. However, each chapter can be read on its own, so the book can be read through like a novel or the reader can be selective and can dip into it wherever he likes. No matter which approach is chosen, it is well worth bearing in mind two things:

1 Any psychology book will be split into chapters, dealing with different aspects of behaviour, but in a human being several kinds of behaviour can be going on at the same time.

2 Individuals' experiences, needs and hopes differ; no book would be able to tell everybody what they want to know. So the reader should constantly ask himself the questions, 'How could this apply to me?' or 'How could I apply this?'

This book is based on the Joint Matriculation Board's (Alternative) Ordinary GCE syllabus in psychology, for which Malcolm Hardy is Chairman of Examiners. It is, however, the result of a joint experience in the teaching of psychology at varied levels in Further Education over several years. Our students have acted as guinea pigs for most of the work in the book; we have been encouraged by their reactions to it, and by the enthusiasm which they seem to have developed for psychology generally. We hope, therefore, that this book will prove to be equally interesting for the general reader, whether it is used for an examination or not.

Our thanks are due to Pamela Hardy, Eileen Heyes, Pam Donoghue and Alice Wragg for typing the manuscript and correcting our spelling mistakes; and to Dave Wilce for some of the diagrams. In addition, we are most grateful for the kind help and assistance given to us by Professor R. L. Gregory, particularly in chapters 2 and 4.

Cheshire, January 1979

Malcolm Hardy
Steve Heyes

Chapter 1

The Biological Bases of Behaviour

The behaviour of any object, whether it is a typewriter, a radio or a human being, must to a great extent depend on its structure. The room in which you are sitting at the moment is full of radio waves, and yet you cannot sense them because your structure is different from that of a radio set. Your picture of the world is different from that of a colour-blind person: he finds it difficult to distinguish between red and green because his eye does not contain some chemical contained by yours. Damage to the brain can cause a grown man to act like a babbling infant or to lose the ability to remember things for more than a few moments. Some drugs act on the brain to give an individual a feeling of elation or depression, anxiety or rage.

Which parts of the brain are responsible for the control of eating, sleeping, and mating? Where are memories stored? How do we form our visual, touch, smell and sound models of the world? These are some of the questions that psychologists are trying to answer in an area of study known as 'physiological psychology' in which the main emphasis is on discovering the structure and functions of the brain and nervous system and of the endocrine system.

The Nerve Cell or Neuron

The basic 'building block' of the brain and nervous system is the *nerve cell* or *neuron*. It is through neurons that information can pass from a sense organ to the brain and from the brain to the muscles. It is estimated that the brain itself consists of about twelve thousand million neurons whose activity makes possible the remarkable range of behaviour and experience that we all share.

Neurons vary in structure but there are three major types – *sensory*, *motor* and *connector neurons*. Sensory neurons carry information to the brain from the sense organs; motor neurons carry information from the brain to the muscles; connector neurons, which are found in the brain and spinal cord, link these two types. The three types consist of a cell body with many branching filaments called *dendrites*; one of these is often very long and is termed the *axon* and it is along this that the nerve impulse travels away from the cell body towards the next neuron in the chain, or to a muscle (see figures 2 and 3). An impulse can be produced by the excitation of a sense organ or the reception of an impulse from another neuron. When an impulse passes along an axon – always in the same direction – the neuron is said to *fire*. The *myelin sheath* around the axon has an insulating effect; it also causes the speed of conduction of the

Figure 1. Uses of Sensory, Motor and Connector Neurons

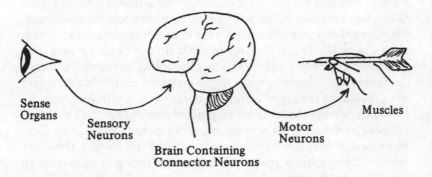

Sense Organs

Sensory Neurons

Brain Containing Connector Neurons

Motor Neurons

Muscles

impulse to be greater than that for neurons without myelin. The speed at which an impulse passes along a neuron may be as fast as 120 metres per second for large-diameter, myelinated axons, or as slow as one metre per second for small-diameter, non-myelinated axons.

The stimulus to the neuron must be large enough to produce an impulse, i.e. it must be above the *threshold of response*; once this threshold is passed the impulse travels without any weakening to the end of the axon. The strength of the impulse in an axon never varies, for it is either present or not; this is known as the *all-or-none rule*. A strong stimulus produces a more rapid burst of impulses than a weaker one; it cannot produce a stronger impulse in an individual neuron, but may stimulate more neurons. After each firing there is a very short period of time, one or two milliseconds, during which

Figure 2. A Sensory Neuron

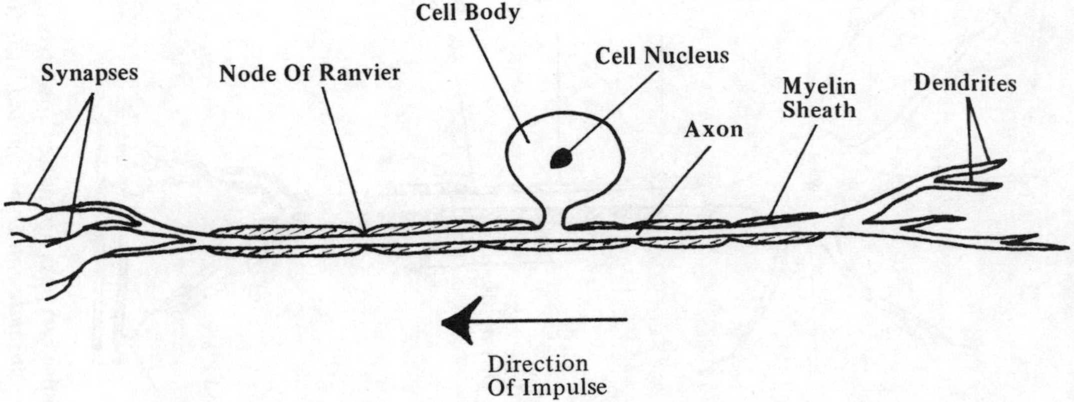

Dendrites

Myelin Sheath

Axon

Cell Nucleus

Cell Body

Node Of Ranvier

Synapses

Direction Of Impulse

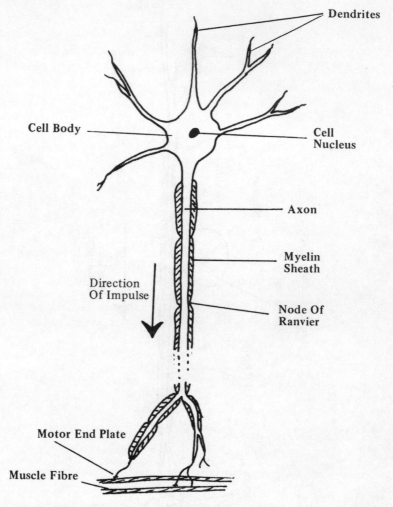

Figure 3. A Motor Neuron

no further impulse can pass no matter how strong the stimulus; this is known as the *absolute refractory period*. It is followed by a short period when the neuron can only be caused to fire by strong stimuli, i.e. the threshold of response is higher than usual; this is known as the *relative refractory period*. Because a strong stimulus can create an impulse as soon as the absolute refractory period is over, it may prompt a firing rate of up to 1,000 impulses per second, whereas the delay caused by the relative refractory period means that the firing rate for a weak stimulus can be as low as 25 impulses per second.

All messages in the nervous system are carried in the form of nerve impulses, but their interpretation depends upon which part of the brain receives the message: in one part an impulse might be interpreted as a spot of light, in another as a sound. Imagine the effect of plugging the nerves from the ear into the visual areas of the brain!

The Motor End Plate

The axons of the motor neurons which terminate on muscles, end in a series of branches. These are tipped by *motor end plates*, each of which is attached to a single muscle fibre. An impulse at the motor end plate causes the muscle to contract, which may thus result in an arm being raised, a movement of the tongue, or any one of thousands of other responses, depending on which muscle is stimulated. Physical activities produced by the stimulation of muscles by nerves are called *motor responses*.

The Synapses

Neurons are not in direct contact with each other; there is a small gap between each cell and its neighbour known as a *synapse* across which the nerve impulse has to pass. When an impulse reaches a *synaptic knob* (see figure 4) it causes the release of chemicals known

Figure 4. A Synapse

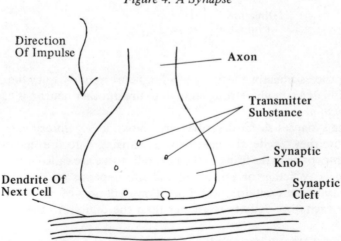

Direction Of Impulse

Axon

Transmitter Substance

Synaptic Knob

Dendrite Of Next Cell

Synaptic Cleft

as *transmitter substances* which pass across the gap, the *synaptic cleft*, and stimulate the next cell. If enough transmitter substance is received the next cell fires. Conduction across a synapse can occur only in one direction.

Many synapses separate each neuron from other neurons; it may be necessary for transmitter substance to be received from several of these synapses at the same time, or from one synapse fired a few times in rapid succession, in order to reach the threshold of response.

Figure 5. *Many Synapses Terminating on One Neuron*

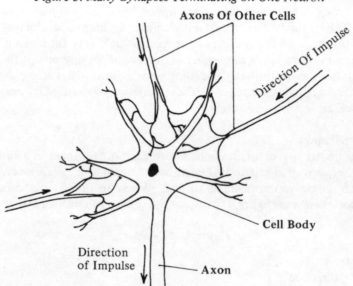

The process whereby the firing of a few neurons adds up to the production of a stimulus strong enough to fire another neuron is called *summation*.

The synapses so far described are known as *excitatory synapses* because they 'excite' the next neuron, causing it to fire, but some synapses prevent the firing of the next cell; these are called *inhibitory synapses*. Whether or not a cell will fire depends on the relative activity of the excitatory and inhibitory synapses of its dendrites: if the excitatory activity is greater than the inhibitory then it will fire.

After a transmitter substance has reached the next neuron it is destroyed and so does not continue to stimulate the cell. Many of the so-called 'nerve gases', produced for warfare, work by preventing the destruction of the transmitter molecules; death results from the continual excitation of many neurons which causes prolonged contraction of all the muscles of the body. The hallucinatory drug LSD is very similar to *serotonin* which is a transmitter substance in some brain synapses; the presence of LSD can thus cause neurons to fire even though no impulses have been passed from the sense organs, which is why LSD takers 'see' things which are not really there.

Inhibitory synapses use different transmitter substances from those used by excitatory synapses and they play an important role in the nervous system. Inhibition controls the spread of excitation through the highly interconnected nervous system and keeps activity channelled in appropriate networks or 'circuits'. Epileptic fits may be due to the excitation of many different brain circuits at the same time. The possible connections with other cells are astronomical in number; the connector neurons in the spine, for example, may each be stimulated by up to two thousand synapses. In chapter 5 on learning, we shall argue that it is changes in the connections between cells in the nervous system that allow both learning and memory.

Methods of Studying the Brain

A simple study of the anatomy of the brain does not tell us very much about the functions of its different parts. However, it might lead us to make educated guesses; for example, if it can be seen that a particular nerve is connected to the retina of the eye and leads towards particular areas of the brain we might guess that that nerve is passing visual information. A lot of information has come from Sir Gordon Holmes' studies of accidental injuries to the brain such as those suffered by soldiers during the First World War. Holmes found that patients with shrapnel lodged in the rear of the brain could not see objects that were placed in some positions in front of the eye. An object moved in front of the eye might be visible then disappear, only to reappear after passing the blind area. This suggested that the rear of the brain dealt with vision. It is difficult to draw conclusions from studies of accidental injury, however, because we may not know exactly where the damage is until the patient dies; nor can we set up an accident and ensure that it will

damage only one part of the brain in order to determine exactly what
caused any change in behaviour that occurs.

Surgical removal of parts of the brain, either by a cut of the knife
or by burning out certain neurons with electrodes, has supplied a
great deal of information about the functions of many parts of the
brain. This technique is known as *ablation*; the idea behind it is that
if, for example, removal of a particular area of the brain leads to

Figure 6. Methods of Studying the Brain

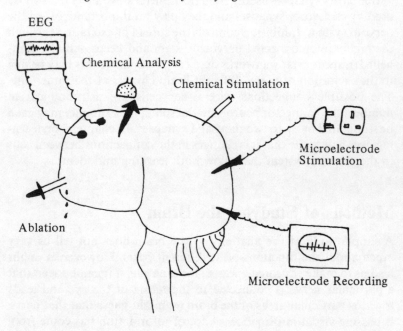

overeating on the part of the subject, then that area must have been
responsible for controlling eating activity. The results of ablation
and other studies have to be considered carefully and in the light
of information from several sources, because the fact that a certain
operation causes a particular change in behaviour does not definitely
prove that the affected part of the brain was the control centre for
that behaviour; the area may simply be one part of a larger system,
or the behaviour change may have been brought about by general
shock to the nervous system.

Other studies involve the insertion of *microelectrodes* – very fine needles which can conduct electricity – into single neurons in the brain. These electrodes may be used either to record the activity of a cell while the animal being studied performs some activity, or to stimulate the cell with a small electric current to gauge the effect of this on behaviour. Chemical studies fall into two similar principal categories – those that analyse the chemicals present in the brain and those in which injected chemicals, often similar to transmitter substances, affect the brain.

For more general studies the *electroencephalogram* or EEG is used to measure the electrical activity of large areas of the brain rather than individual neurons. Characteristic patterns of brain activity are found during different kinds of behaviour, for example when the subject is active, relaxed or dreaming.

To summarize then: the major physiological methods of approach to the study of the brain are anatomy, accident, ablation, electrical and chemical analysis, electrical and chemical stimulation, and recording of the activity of larger parts of the brain.

The Nervous System

The cell bodies of most neurons are contained within the brain or spinal cord. The elongated axons of many neurons pass information either in from the sense organs or out to the muscles. Some of these axons are over one metre in length; they are grouped in bundles known as *nerves*, which are usually large enough to see with the naked eye in a dissected animal. Those leaving the brain or spinal cord through holes in the skull are known as *cranial nerves*; others situated between the vertebrae of the spine are called *spinal nerves*. Most contain both motor and sensory neurons.

The brain and spinal cord contain the majority of cell bodies and are therefore termed collectively the *central nervous system* or CNS; the nerve fibres outside the brain and spine are known as the *peripheral nervous system*.

The Peripheral Nervous System
The peripheral nervous system consists of two main sections, which have different structures and functions – the *somatic nervous system* and the *autonomic nervous system* or ANS.

The Somatic Nervous System

The somatic nervous system comprises the nerves that carry impulses from the sense organs – the eyes, ears, nose, tongue and skin – and that affect those muscles which are under voluntary control. Any part of the body that you can move of your own volition, such as your fingers or face, is therefore controlled by the somatic section of the nervous system. The cell bodies of these neurons are mostly contained in the central nervous system; only those axons with a myelin sheath are present in the periphery.

The Autonomic Nervous System or ANS

The autonomic nervous system controls the internal organs and glands of the body – those activities which require no conscious effort, for example heartbeat, blood-pressure and pupil size. You cannot decide to alter the size of your eyes' pupils because they are not under voluntary control (although you could of course do so indirectly by looking towards a bright light). 'Autonomic' axons do not have thick myelin sheaths and the cell bodies are outside the central nervous system.

There are two sections of the ANS, the *sympathetic* and the *parasympathetic divisions*, both of which connect with most of the glands and organs of the body, usually with opposing results, for example impulses in the sympathetic system cause an increase in heart-rate but impulses in the parasympathetic system cause a decrease in heart-rate.

The ANS is important in emotional experience and its action can produce in the body what Walter Cannon described as the *fight-or-flight syndrome*. When you are in a threatening or stressful situation the sympathetic section of the ANS becomes active, increasing blood flow to the brain and muscles so that these organs can function more effectively; at the same time, the bronchioles of the lungs are dilated so that more oxygen can be taken into the bloodstream. In such situations the action of the sympathetic nervous system also inhibits bodily processes which are not needed to prepare for action, such as digestion. Thus when the sympathetic nervous system is active the body is excellently tuned either to stay and fight or to flee, hence Cannon's term. The effects of the sympathetic system can be quite long-lasting because it also causes the adrenal glands to secrete *adrenalin* into the bloodstream. Adrenalin is very similar to the transmitter substances in the sympathetic synapses: it induces increased firing in the sympathetic nervous system. For this reason you may feel your heart beating heavily for several moments after a dangerous situation, such as a near accident in a car, has passed.

The parasympathetic division of the ANS controls the conservation and restoration of the body's energy resources; because its effect is normally opposite to that of the sympathetic system most of the organs and glands are controlled by a balance of the two systems.

Consider someone wandering round an isolated, dimly-lit country house. Suddenly there is a sound of creaking floorboards and the

Some of the Functions of the ANS Showing the Opposing Action of the Sympathetic and Parasympathetic Sections

Organ Or Gland	Effect of Sympathetic Action	Effect of Parasympathetic Action
Heart	Heart-beat increased	Heart-beat decreased
Liver	Sugar released into blood	Sugar stored
Intestines	Peristalsis (muscular action causing food to move along intestine) slowed	Peristalsis accelerated
Salivary Gland	Secretion suppressed	Secretion stimulated
Pupil of eye	Dilated	Contracted
Bladder	Relaxed	Constricted

candles blow out. At this moment his autonomic nervous system is highly active, especially the sympathetic section: his heart beats faster; his blood-pressure rises; his mouth feels dry; the pupils of his eyes dilate; the blood vessels serving the voluntary muscles of his trunk and limbs enlarge; the blood vessels to his stomach and intestines become smaller; and contractions of the stomach and in-testines cease or may even be reversed. In addition the *galvanic skin response* – the electrical resistance of the skin – will decrease due to the greater production of sweat. (This galvanic skin response or GSR may be measured by a simple battery-operated device known as a GSR meter.) He experiences a strong emotion of fear. Imagine, on

The Relationship and Functions of the Parts of the Nervous System

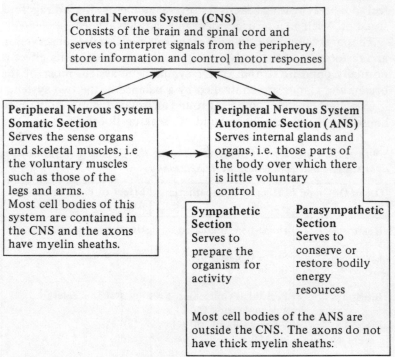

Central Nervous System (CNS)
Consists of the brain and spinal cord and
serves to interpret signals from the periphery,
store information and control motor responses

Peripheral Nervous System
Somatic Section
Serves the sense organs
and skeletal muscles, i.e
the voluntary muscles
such as those of the
legs and arms.
Most cell bodies of this
system are contained in
the CNS and the axons
have myelin sheaths.

Peripheral Nervous System
Autonomic Section (ANS)
Serves internal glands and
organs, i.e. those parts of
the body over which there
is little voluntary
control

Sympathetic
Section
Serves to
prepare the
organism for
activity

Parasympathetic
Section
Serves to
conserve or
restore bodily
energy
resources

Most cell bodies of the ANS are
outside the CNS. The axons do not
have thick myelin sheaths:

the other hand, that a friend has died. Again your autonomic nervous system is active but this time it will be predominantly the parasympathetic division; you experience the emotion of sadness. With other emotions such as anger and joy both sections of the autonomic nervous system may be highly active.

The James–Lange Theory of Emotion Many of the physiological changes that occur during strong emotion are easily noticeable to the person experiencing the emotion but others such as redirection of blood flow are not. One question which has intrigued psychologists for many years is that of the relationship between physiological changes and the experience of emotion. Towards the end of the last century W. James and C. Lange put forward theories which seemed to run contrary to common sense. They suggested that when someone is confronted by an unpleasant situation this causes activity in the autonomic nervous system; that sensory nerves transmit information to the brain about the changes in his physiological state; and that the brain interprets these messages as a feeling of emotion. The feeling of emotion occurs after the bodily changes, according to the James–Lange theory. James said, 'We feel sorry because we cry, we feel afraid because we run.'

The James–Lange Theory of Emotion

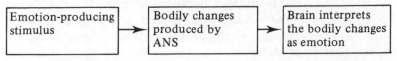

Real-life experiences sometimes back up the James–Lange theory: in a near accident your heart beats fast and you may then feel anxiety, but this feeling will occur only after the danger has passed. However, this theory is not true for all cases of emotion. If it were, the changes which accompany happiness, joy, pleasure, sadness, anxiety, fear and anger would have to differ noticeably in order for us to be able to distinguish these kinds of emotion from each other. But in general our awareness of bodily changes is not very great; physiological studies seem to have found that while some emotions, such as anger and sadness, show different physical changes, in many emotions they are quite similar. However, this lack of evidence for physical changes in emotion is not proof; it may well be that we do not yet have measuring instruments which are sensitive enough to measure tiny changes which may be important.

Cannon's Theory of Emotion In the 1920s W. Cannon suggested that bodily changes and feelings of emotion were independent of each other; that the brain experienced emotion as a direct result of perception of the external world; and that the external situation caused

Cannon's Theory of Emotion

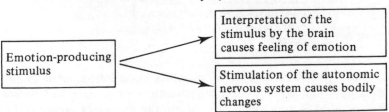

bodily changes by stimulating lower regions of the brain which activate the autonomic nervous system.

Schachter and Singer's Theory of Emotion In the 1960s S. Schachter and J. E. Singer put forward a theory which emphasizes the role of the brain in interpreting situations that cause emotion. They argued that people may feel different emotions despite similarities in the accompanying bodily changes because the brain forms different interpretations of the stimulus which caused the changes; thus when someone nearly falls downstairs he interprets his feelings as anxiety or fear because of his knowledge of stairs and the effects of falling, whereas the same physiological changes in another situation would lead him to experience a different emotion. The brain's ability to differentiate according to the situation can be observed when people change their bodily state by drinking alcohol: in a party atmosphere the emotion felt may be happiness but in an unpleasant atmosphere it may be depression. In both cases, however, the alcohol has the same physiological effects.

Schachter and Singer do not say that bodily changes and the experience of emotion are independent as Cannon argued, or that the physiological changes cause the feeling of emotion as proposed by James and Lange, but that the experience of emotion depends both upon physiological changes and interpretation of external events.

Schachter and Singer's Theory of Emotion

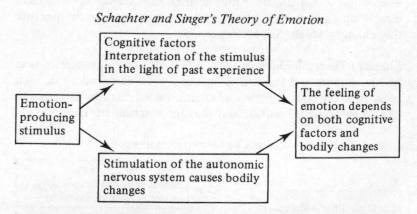

Cognitive factors include all those factors – perception, memory and thinking – that influence the interpretation of stimuli. Sometimes the cognitive factors alone can initiate the feeling of emotion, for example if you suddenly remember that you were asked to hand in an essay to your tutor today but you have failed to write it; this might cause an increase in the activity of your ANS. Bodily changes such as increased heart-rate would occur and you would experience the emotion of anxiety.

The perception of bodily changes can affect the extent to which emotions are felt. In 1966 G. W. Hohmann interviewed subjects who had damage to the spine which severely limited the amount of information their brains received about changes occurring in the body, and he found that although they still felt emotions, these emotions were not felt to the same extent as before their accidents. Without information of bodily changes the subjects felt less intense emotion.

In 1962 Schachter and Singer provided support for their theory with the results of an experiment which, by injecting subjects with adrenalin, involved the production of the physiological changes which normally accompany emotion. They found that the increased heart-rate, flushed face and trembling hands caused by the adrenalin were interpreted in different ways depending upon the information available to the subjects. These subjects were told that they had been injected with a vitamin compound. Each was then put into a room with another person who was actually a confederate of the experimenter and was scripted to act in either a happy or an angry fashion: he was known as the 'stooge subject'. Schachter and Singer found that subjects accompanied by a happy stooge interpreted their bodily changes as an emotion of happiness, whereas those accompanied by an angry stooge felt angry. Another group of subjects were informed of the physiological side-effects of the drug; these subjects were not affected by the behaviour of the stooges. Such results support the theory that the interpretation of the bodily changes that occur with emotion depend largely on the cognitive interpretation of the situation.

The preceding theories of emotion therefore give different accounts of the effect of the autonomic nervous system on behaviour: James and Lange suggested that autonomic activity causes the feeling of emotion through its effect on bodily changes and thus has an effect on the changes in behaviour that accompany emotion; Cannon argued that it simply prepares the animal for fight or flight but does not cause the feeling of emotion; and more recent theories, like those of Schachter and Singer, suggest that in triggering bodily changes the autonomic nervous system affects the strength with which the emotion is felt but that the type of emotion felt depends on cognitive factors, which are the responsibility of the central nervous system.

The Central Nervous System or CNS
The CNS consists of the brain and spinal cord; it is believed to contain not only some twelve thousand million neurons but ten times as many *glial cells*, which fill the spaces between neurons and probably supply them with nutrient and their myelin sheaths. R. Thompson maintains that the number of possible interconnections between the cells of a single human brain is greater than the number of atomic particles that constitute the entire universe.

At birth the brain contains the adult number of neurons but weighs only half that of an adult brain. By the age of two and a half the brain reaches 75 per cent of its adult weight; it is during these early years that the brain is most vulnerable to the effect of malnutrition, according to J. Dobbing and G. Sands. The average weight of the adult brain is 1250 grams for females and 1375 grams for males; it increases in weight after birth because of the multiplication of glial cells, the process of myelination of axons and an increase in the number of interconnections and the size of neurons. Brain size itself does not reflect intelligence and neither, it seems, does the ratio of brain weight to body weight; what seems to be important is the number of *cortical neurons* and the connections between them. (Cortical neurons are the nerve cells in the *cortex*, the area forming the surface of the top part of the brain, which is responsible for processes such as thinking and memory.)

If the central nervous system simply provided direct connections between sense organs and muscles, the number of responses to any situation would be extremely limited; the same response would always be elicited by the same stimulus. However, the connection is not direct; there are both excitatory and inhibitory synapses in the system, which act like switches, so that a particular stimulus may trigger one pathway in a particular situation, but if that pathway is being inhibited for some reason, it may trigger a different pathway.

This characteristic of indirectly linking sensation and response means that most animals – and humans – have a huge behavioural repertoire and can produce different responses to the same stimulus. For example, the smell of baking bread may make you feel very

Figure 7. The Brain

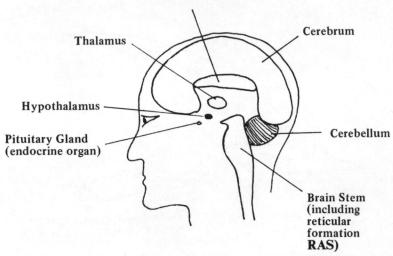

hungry one day, but the next day – perhaps because you are not hungry, or have had a severe fright – it may make you feel sick.

Figure 7 shows the parts of the central nervous system, each of which has a slightly different function. It appears that the lower sections deal with simple automatic behaviour such as reflexes, control of breathing and digestion, and the passage of information to higher centres in the brain. The higher centres of the brain control complex voluntary behaviour and it is here that processes such as thinking and remembering occur.

The Spinal Cord

The *spinal cord* is about the thickness of a little finger and passes from the brain stem down the whole length of the back encased in the vertebrae of the backbone. This cord connects the central and peripheral nervous systems, providing a pathway between the brain and the body. Some of the very simplest reactions to stimuli, the *reflexes* – the reactions you give when you quickly pull your hand away from a hot object or when your knee jerks in response to the doctor's hammer – are controlled by the spinal cord. Reflexes are extremely primitive items of behaviour because they are involuntary and always take the same form given the same stimulus; yet because

Figure 8. A Simple Reflex Arc

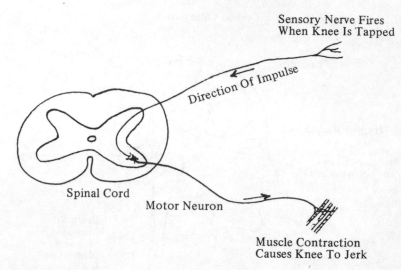

they are so fast they can prevent the sort of damage we might do ourselves if, for example, we did not let go of a hot object until nerve impulses had been transmitted to the brain, processed and then passed down again.

In the knee-jerk reflex a sensory neuron fires when the correct part of the knee is tapped; this message passes into the spine where the synapse of the sensory neuron transmits the impulse to a motor neuron. The firing of this causes the knee muscle to contract and the leg to jerk forward. Most reflexes involve a connector neuron between the sensory and motor neuron; this simple system of connection is known as a *reflex arc*. The two or three neurons of the reflex arc do, however, have synapses with others which pass up and down the spine and it is through these pathways that we actually become aware of the reflex.

The Brain Stem

The lower part of the brain, which is linked to the spinal cord, contains structures with a variety of functions. However, one of its main purposes is to control those kinds of internal behaviour over which we have little or no voluntary control, such as breathing, heartbeat and digestion. One structure of the *brain stem*, the *reticular formation*, which is sometimes known as the *Reticular Activating System* or RAS, has connections with the whole of the cortex and receives stimulation from the sense organs. It is thought to be important in the maintenance of wakefulness and attention in the cortex; many sleeping pills therefore work by restraining its activity.

The Cerebellum

The *cerebellum* is involved in the maintenance of balance and the performance of skilled actions like walking or riding a bicycle, and similarly aids the co-ordination of flight in birds and of swimming in fish. The cerebellum thus allows us to perform complicated actions 'without thinking'; if it were damaged such activities would require great concentration and might even become impossible. People with damage to the cerebellum display a noticeable loss of muscle control.

The Hypothalamus

This structure, no bigger than the top part of a little finger, has an essential role to play in the motivation of behaviour. The *hypothalamus* is extremely well supplied with blood and contains neurons which are sensitive to changes in blood temperature and content. A fall in the amount of sugar in the blood causes part of the hypothalamus to become active in passing impulses to the cortex which may prompt the person or animal to search for something to eat; at the same time impulses are transmitted to other parts of the nervous system and to the pituitary gland, causing physiological changes such as the release of sugar from the liver into the blood (see page 25). The process of maintaining a fairly constant level of blood temperature, sugar and salt concentration, hormones and so on is known as *homeostasis*; without it we would not be able to survive. Electrical stimulation and ablation studies have shown that the hypothalamus plays an important part in controlling the activity of the autonomic nervous system and emotion.

The Thalamus

The *thalamus* is a relay station for nerve pathways leading to and from the cortex. The impulses passed to the cortex concern sensory information such as vision and hearing; those passing down are directed towards the cerebellum and concern complex limb movements. Another part of the thalamus influences sleep and wakefulness.

The Limbic System

This lies just below the cerebral hemispheres (see the following section) and consists of a collection of individual structures involved in motivation, emotion and memory. Ablation of various parts of this system in monkeys can result in either an increase or a decrease in aggressive behaviour, while damage to other parts in humans has been shown to limit severely the length of time for which a patient is able to remember new material. Nerve pathways link the limbic system with both the thalamus and the hypothalamus.

The Cerebrum and the Cortex

On examination of the surface of the brain the most striking feature is the extremely wrinkled surface of the *cerebrum*, which is split by a large crevice from front to rear suggesting the appearance of a walnut. The two *cerebral hemispheres*, one on each side of the crevice, are joined by a mass of nervous tissue called the *corpus callosum*. Although the cerebral hemispheres are the largest structures of the brain the most important part, the cortex, consists only of the top few layers of cells; it is here that control of intelligent behaviour largely originates. The major concerns of the cortex are perception, learning and memory and control of motor functions. In humans the cortex also controls the production and understanding of language.

The wrinkled surface of the cerebrum appears to be divided into four lobes as shown in figure 9, and some forms of behaviour can

Figure 9. Lobes of the Cerebrum

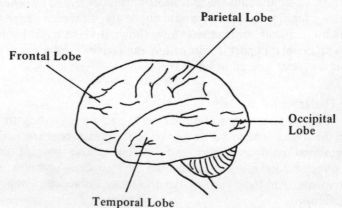

Figure 10a. The Area of Cortex Dealing with Muscle Control and Bodily Feeling

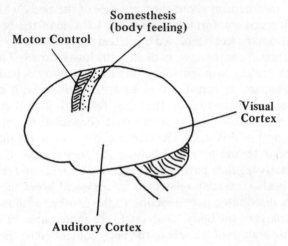

Figure 10b. The Area of Cortex Dealing with Bodily Feeling

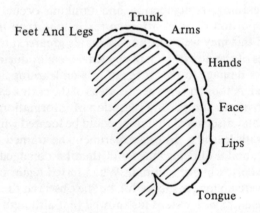

be localized to particular areas on those lobes. The *visual cortex* is found in the *occipital lobe*, and cells in this area receive input from the light-sensitive cells of the eyes' retinas. The *auditory cortex* in the *temporal lobe* receives information from the ear. There is a strip of cortex at the front of the *parietal lobe*; this receives input from all over the body and when a part the body is touched it is stimulated and produces some sort of sensation. The sense of bodily feeling with which this area is involved is known as *somesthesis*. This strip of cortex is organized so that the strip on the left hemisphere receives information about the right side of the body while that on the right receives information from the left side of the body. Information from the feet is received by cells at the top of the strip whereas information from the face is dealt with lower down. The amount of cortex dealing with particular parts of the body depends not on the size but on the sensitivity of an area. Patients with damage to this strip of the cortex report that they feel as though they have lost part of their bodies. In mice the cells connected to the whiskers occupy most of this strip. The motor control strip lies just in front of the body-feeling area and behind the *frontal lobe*. Cells in this strip directly regulate particular muscle movements and their organization is also inversely related to the physical areas they control. They are distributed in proportion to the number of muscles in the various parts of the body. Damage to the motor area of the cortex results in paralysis of the area of the body controlled by the damaged part.

A large proportion of the cortex in man does not have a sensory or motor function; this is called the *association cortex* where the processes of learning, remembering and thinking occur. There is a greater proportion of association cortex in man than in any other animal and this may well account for man's greater intelligence.

In a series of classic experiments by Karl Lashley during the 1920s the effects of damage to the cortex of rats on learning and memory were studied. Although very specific areas of the cortex can be shown to deal with motor control and reception of information from sense organs Lashley discovered that none could be located which specifically dealt with learning. In one experiment he trained rats to find their way round a difficult maze and then he damaged fifteen per cent of the cortex in each animal. When tested again on the maze these rats were no longer successful, but he observed that they could re-learn the maze with ease. This showed that although one area of the cortex was used for learning the maze in the first instance a different area could do the same job. Lashley coined the *Law of Mass Action* which states that for the learning of difficult problems the effect of cortical damage depends upon the amount, and not the position, of the damage: the more cortex affected, the more difficulty the rat has in learning the maze.

Language, the ability to communicate with words, is a peculiarly human ability and possibly originates from certain specialized areas of the cortex on the left hemisphere. A sharp blow on the left of the head might result in an inability to understand or produce the spoken word, whereas a blow on the right would not.

In 1865 Paul Broca found that patients with damage to the part of the brain now known as *Broca's Area* (see figure 11) lost their ability to speak properly although they could still move tongue, jaws and vocal cords. The speech of such patients is very slow and crude: instead of producing full sentences they tend to miss out small words

Figure 11. Language Areas of the Brain

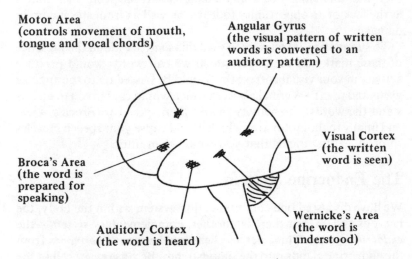

Motor Area
(controls movement of mouth, tongue and vocal chords)

Angular Gyrus
(the visual pattern of written words is converted to an auditory pattern)

Visual Cortex
(the written word is seen)

Broca's Area
(the word is prepared for speaking)

Auditory Cortex
(the word is heard)

Wernicke's Area
(the word is understood)

and the endings of nouns and verbs. When asked what he did the previous night a patient might reply 'Go... cinema.' It appears that Broca's Area is necessary to prepare words for speaking but not for understanding them; such patients have no difficulty in comprehending. Behind Broca's Area, however, is a part of the cortex known as *Wernicke's Area*, damage to which does prevent a person from understanding language; nevertheless he may still be able to hear and enjoy music. While damage to Wernicke's Area does not prevent talking the patient may forget some words and substitute others: he may ask for a pen by saying 'Please pass the thing you write with.' Damage to Wernicke's Area causes problems in the understanding of both written and spoken language; damage to another area, the *angular gyrus*, causes the loss of reading ability whilst having no effect on comprehension of the spoken word. Patients with damage to the angular gyrus are able to see the written word but it has no meaning for them; it has been suggested that this part of the cortex must therefore convert the visual patterns of the written word into auditory patterns which are then passed along to Wernicke's Area for comprehension.

Psychologists sometimes study the performance of a person in the production or comprehension of language in order to help them locate specific areas of damage to the brain which might have resulted from an accident or tumour. It must be remembered, however, that an inability to use language may result from such things as the lack of an opportunity to learn, as well as from specific brain damage.

To summarize, if you were to read this sentence aloud the presence of these marks on the paper which we call words would produce activity in your visual cortex; this would be passed on to the angular gyrus and then to Wernicke's Area which would enable you to understand the words; the activity would then spread to Broca's Area, and finally to the motor area which would cause your speech muscles to produce the sounds that you would then utter.

The Endocrine System

We have discussed one communication system within the body, the nervous system, but there is another, complementary system – the *endocrine system*. This releases chemicals known as *hormones* from the endocrine glands into the bloodstream. Because every cell in the body is either directly or indirectly in contact with the blood system, hormones can reach every cell, whereas nerves only pass messages to the muscles and from the sense organs. As the messages of the endocrine system pass in the bloodstream this system is obviously slower than the nervous system, which can pass messages in a matter of milliseconds; but it is more suited to transmitting steady, relatively unchanging messages over a long period of time. Behaviour such as catching a cup before it falls to the floor and smashes must be controlled by the nervous system because of the need for speed. On the other hand behaviour demonstrating an increased inclination for courtship during certain months of the year in birds and other animals has a hormonal basis.

The endocrine system consists of the glands shown in figure 12. The pituitary is known as the master gland because it releases hormones which in turn stimulate the other glands to produce their own hormones.

The pituitary gland is connected by many nerve pathways to the hypothalamus; the nervous and endocrine systems closely interact to control the functioning of the body. This interaction takes place, for example, when someone has not had anything to drink for a while. The fall in liquid content of the blood is registered by the

Figure 12. The Endocrine System

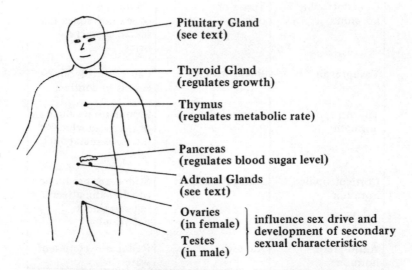

Pituitary Gland
(see text)

Thyroid Gland
(regulates growth)

Thymus
(regulates metabolic rate)

Pancreas
(regulates blood sugar level)

Adrenal Glands
(see text)

Ovaries
(in female)

Testes
(in male)

influence sex drive and development of secondary sexual characteristics

hypothalamus; it sends nerve impulses to the cortex which interprets the message as a feeling of thirst and may prompt the person to look for something to drink. At the same time the hypothalamus passes impulses to the pituitary gland; this releases an antidiuretic hormone which controls the extent to which water is reabsorbed into the blood from the kidneys after blood filtration; this in turn causes less water to be excreted into the bladder. The combined actions of the cortex and the pituitary gland therefore produce a reaction to water deficiency on both a behavioural and a physiological level.

The endocrine and nervous systems also interact in stressful situations (see page 189 on stress). As seen, the sympathetic section of the ANS is highly active when we are under pressure, producing the fight-or-flight syndrome and mobilizing all the body's emergency energy resources. The adrenal glands are caused to secrete adrenalin and *noradrenalin* into the bloodstream; because these are the transmitter substances for the sympathetic nervous system they have the same effect on the organs of the body, maintaining the fight-or-flight syndrome.

Some Pituitary Hormones and their Effects

Hormone	Stimulates	Effect
Growth hormone	Body tissues	Increases growth
Gonadotrophic hormone	Testes or ovaries	Stimulates production of sex hormones and sexual characteristics
Vasopressin	Blood vessels	Causes the blood vessels to contract
Thyrotrophic hormone	Thyroid gland	Stimulates production of thyroxin which increases metabolic rate
Corticotrophic hormone	Adrenal gland	Stimulates production of adrenalin affecting emotional behaviour
Antidiuretic hormone	Kidneys	Reduces excretion of water

The adrenal glands have two parts – the *adrenal medulla*, which secretes adrenalin and noradrenalin, and the *adrenal cortex*, which secretes a range of other hormones. One of these is *hydrocortisone*, which functions to adjust the level of sugar stored in the liver after the amount has fallen because of stress (see page 189 for a consideration of stress).

Female cats that have not been neutered 'come on heat' about three times a year and then attract and accept willing males, yet at other times a male that comes too close encounters only hostility. The chain of reaction during the 'heat' periods starts with the production of *follicle-stimulating hormone* in the pituitary gland which stimulates the growth of eggs and the production of *oestrogen* by the ovaries. The presence of oestrogen in the bloodstream causes changes in the reproductive system, such as thickening of the uterus walls; it also stimulates the hypothalamus which, in connection with other parts of the nervous system, prompts the female to lift her rump, move her tail to one side and make treading movements with her rear legs when a male appears. The stimulus to the nervous system during copulation reaches the hypothalamus and is passed on to the cat's pituitary gland; this then releases *luteinizing hormone* which effects the release from the ovaries of eggs to be fertilized by the male's sperm.

Thus sexual activity in animals is also governed by the action of the endocrine and nervous systems in conjunction, to cause both physiological and behavioural changes.

Summary

1 The nervous system consists of millions of neurons connected by excitatory and inhibitory synapses.
2 Each neuron has a threshold of response and once stimulation exceeds this it fires. The firing obeys the all-or-none rule.
3 The firing of a neuron is followed by the absolute and then the relative refractory periods.
4 Physiological psychologists have used various methods of studying the brain – anatomy, accident, ablation, microelectrode recording and stimulation, and chemical analysis and stimulation.
5 The central nervous system (CNS) consists of the brain and spinal cord. The peripheral nervous system consists of the somatic nervous system which passes messages in from the sense organs and out to the voluntary muscles, and the autonomic nervous system (ANS) which deals with emotions and involuntary functions. The autonomic nervous system has two sections, the sympathetic and parasympathetic.
6 Activity of the sympathetic nervous system puts the body into the fight-or-flight syndrome.
7 The James–Lange theory suggests that changes in the body produced by autonomic activity cause feelings of emotion.
8 Cannon argued that the activity of the autonomic nervous system occurs at the same time as feelings of emotion but does not cause them.

9 Schachter and Singer argued that the feeling of emotion depends on an interaction between physiological factors which determine degree of emotion and cognitive factors which determine type of emotion.

10 The parts of the central nervous system perform different functions: the spinal cord is responsible for reflexes and the transmission of messages from brain to body; the brain stem including the reticular formation affects wakefulness and attention; the cerebellum enables balance and the co-ordination of skilled actions; the hypothalamus governs motivation and emotion; the thalamus acts as a relay station between the sense organs, the cortex and the cerebellum; the limbic system influences motivation, memory and emotion; and the surface of the cerebrum, the cortex, controls intelligent behaviour.

11 Functions such as visual and auditory awareness, bodily feeling, motor control and language control, are related to specific regions of the cortex.

12 Lashley showed that no specific region of the association cortex is involved in learning and memory of specific behaviour.

13 The endocrine system affects the state of the body by the release of hormones. Its effects are slower but more long-lasting than those of the nervous system.

14 Both nervous and endocrine systems are important in the control of, among other things, thirst, emotion and sexual activity.

Chapter 2

Sensory Information Processing

The brain cannot deal directly with light, nor with sound waves. It can deal only with information in the form of electrical impulses. It is therefore the function of all sense organs to translate physical information – light or sound waves, for example – into electrical impulses. This translation, or *transduction*, means that for each type of external stimulus there must be an electrical impulse code. This section looks at how transduction occurs, and what routes the coded information takes to the brain. Only the two major systems, vision and hearing, will be described here, but the same general procedures occur for all sensory information.

However, before the research in these areas is described a very important point must be made. The physiology of vision and hearing shows how coded electrical 'pictures' of the outside world reach the brain; but we know that once there, this information is reorganized and interpreted by the brain. The pictures entering the eye are usually not exactly the same as the finished perception. As a result of previous learning, motivation and emotion, the same retinal image may be interpreted in different ways at different times by the same individual.

As an example, imagine taking a walk in the country with a biologist and a geologist. The biologist might see many kinds of plants and flowers, while you might just see a mass of greenery; the geologist might see escarpments and moraines where you can only see hills. Their previous learning and different interests will have enabled them to extract much more information from their retinal images than you could. But because their interests are different – biological events versus geological – they will each have extracted different information from their retinal images.

The Visual System

There are three main processes which take place in the visual system – coding, transmission and decoding of visual information.

Coding takes place at the *retina* of the eye. The retina is made up of two kinds of specialized, light-sensitive cells called *rods* and *cones*.

Rods
These cells are mainly responsible for vision in low levels of light, and at the edges of the retina. They do not signal colours, and give only black-and-white vision.

Cones
These are responsible for colour vision and fine-detail vision. The small region of the retina which gives the most detailed vision, the centre of the *fovea*, consists entirely of cones. However, cones only work well in good illumination; at night, or in low levels of illumination, the cones are not effective and the rods take over. This is why one does not see much colour at night.

The image on the retina has several characteristics – brightness, colour, shape and movement. These characteristics of the retinal image are coded as patterns of electrical impulses which contain all this information coded by layers of cells in the retina.

Brightness
Individual retinal cells code brightness in a simple way: the brighter the illumination, the more frequently the cells fire.

Colour
Colour is coded only by the cones. Any colour is made up of three primary colours – red, blue and green. In the retina, there are three corresponding types of cones – red sensitive, blue sensitive and green sensitive. Each of these has an individual pattern of firing (see figure 14). Any colour falling on the retina is composed of different amounts of these colours; turquoise might be 70 per cent blue, 30 per cent green. Consequently if the retina were to be presented with a turquoise image the blue cones would be firing fairly fast, the green fairly slowly, and the red not at all. Thus the brain receives the electrical signals – 70 per cent blue, 30 per cent green – and fits them together to interpret the colour as turquoise.

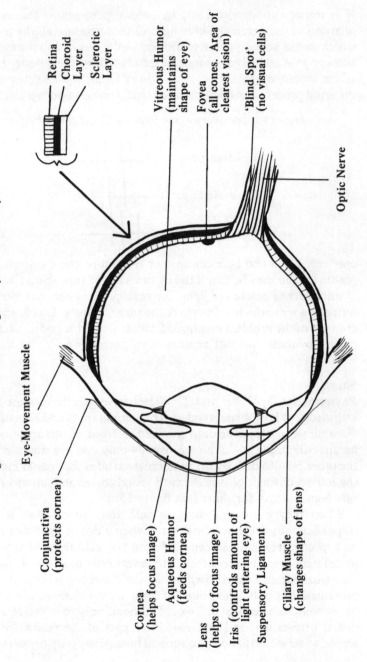

Figure 13. Cross-sectional Diagram of the Human Eye

Retina
Choroid Layer
Sclerotic Layer

Vitreous Humor (maintains shape of eye)

Fovea (all cones. Area of clearest vision)

'Blind Spot' (no visual cells)

Optic Nerve

Eye-Movement Muscle

Conjunctiva (protects cornea)

Cornea (helps focus image)

Aqueous Humor (feeds cornea)

Lens (helps to focus image)

Iris (controls amount of light entering eye)

Suspensory Ligament

Ciliary Muscle (changes shape of lens)

It is important to note that, in colour perception, the various mixtures of red, green and blue light cannot produce all the colours which we can actually perceive. For example, brown and the metallic colours gold and silver cannot be produced by the simple mixing of the coloured lights. However, Edwin Land, the inventor of the Polaroid process, has demonstrated that a colour photograph using

Figure 14. Imaginary Cone Impulse Codes for Colour

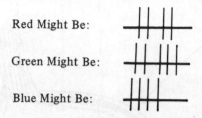

Red Might Be:

Green Might Be:

Blue Might Be:

only red, green and blue can in fact reproduce these colours. The reason for this may be that if the pictures are of real objects, instead of unpatterned patches of light, the perceptual system has more information with which to interpret the three colours. This is another example of the problem mentioned earlier – that the coded electrical picture by itself does not explain all of perception.

Shape

Physiologists D. Hubel and T. Wiesel have greatly increased our knowledge of how shape is coded. They shone spots and bars of light via a filmstrip projector onto a screen in front of the open eyes of an anaesthetized cat – although usually only one eye was used and the other blindfolded. By using microelectrodes they could monitor the activity of single cells in the cat's visual cortex and *lateral geniculate body*, or LGB for short (see figure 15b).

When they monitored an LGB cell, they found that it only responded – by firing at a fast rate – when a dot of light was shone on a specific area of the screen. Different LGB cells responded to dots in different areas of the screen. However, cells near the surface of the visual cortex – called *simple cells* – did not fire when dots were presented, but only when lines of light were shone on the screen. Moreover, each cortical cell would respond only to a line at a particular orientation, and in a particular part of the retina. For example, some would fire only to vertical lines, some only to horizontal lines, some to diagonal lines, and so on, for a full 360 degrees. Deeper in the visual cortex were yet more cells – called *complex cells* – which each responded to a bar of light in a specific orientation, but would do so when the line was in nearly any area of the screen.

From these rather complicated findings, an important idea emerges – that there are 'feature-detecting' mechanisms in the visual

Figure 15a. Links between Receptive Fields and the Visual Cortex

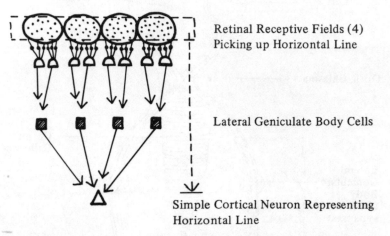

Retinal Receptive Fields (4) Picking up Horizontal Line

Lateral Geniculate Body Cells

Simple Cortical Neuron Representing Horizontal Line

system which analyse the visual image for outlines and shapes. Hubel and Wiesel proposed that each LGB cell receives impulses from a roughly circular group of retinal cells – rods or cones – which are known as the *receptive field* of the LGB cell. Different receptive fields send impulses to different LGB cells, whose receptive fields happen to be arranged in a straight line on the retina (see figure 15a). Only when most of these LGB cells have fired will the simple cortical cell fire – and the only stimulus which will cause the LGB cells to fire is a bar of light in a particular orientation and in a specific position on the retina. Complex cortical cells presumably have inputs from several simple cortical cells, each of which represents the same orientation of line, but at different positions on the retina. If any of these cells fire, the complex cell is likely to fire too; thus it is sensitive to the orientation of line only, irrespective of its position on the retina.

The visual cortex is organized in horizontal layers, but with vertical columns penetrating them. It seems that cells on the surface of these columns represent simple but specific visual information, while cells in successively deeper levels respond more generally to visual features. (Hubel and Wiesel reported that they found a cell, deep in one of these columns, which would only fire when the monkey's

Figure 15b. Diagrammatic View of Human Visual Pathways

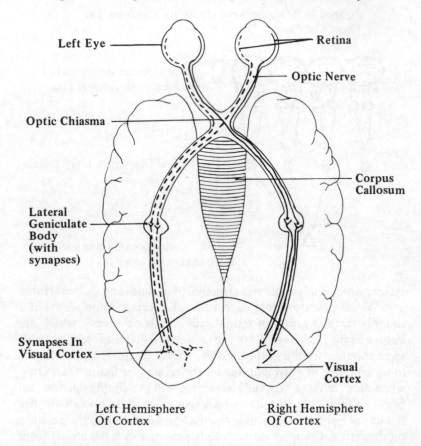

hand was in view.) Perhaps deeper levels introduce links with other areas of the brain involving memory, other senses, and so on. In other words, although simple information seems to be represented by cells on the surface of the cortex, deeper into the cortex more and more information from other sources is collated, to produce our visual model of the world.

Figure 16. Possible Connections between Complex Cortical Cells and Cells in Deeper Levels of the Cortex (Hypercomplex Cells)

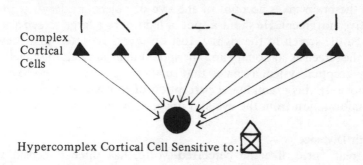

Movement

When the eye is stationary the image of a moving object passes across the receptive fields of many cortical cells. Movement can then be coded by the passage of excitation from one cell to another and also by some cortical cells which only fire when an object passes in a particular direction across its receptive field. The detection of movement is, however, more complicated than this since images pass across the retina when the eye is moved and yet movement of the eye does not cause the world to appear to move in front of the observer. The reason for this appears to be that as nerve impulses pass from the brain to the eye muscles they also act on the movement-perception system, so that when the command is made to move the eyes, this also counteracts the effect of images passing across the receptive fields; these are perceived as static if they move in the opposite direction to the eye at a speed similar to that of the eye. An image that remains on the same spot of the retina while the eye moves is perceived as moving, hence we can follow an object with our eyes and perceive it as moving in relation to its background.

The brain can compensate for the fact that the whole body is moving in the analysis of images moving across the retina so that a driver perceives the road as still while he moves along. Confusion sometimes occurs when inadequate information is available, for example when looking out of a carriage window at a station it can be difficult to decide whether it is your train or the one adjacent that has started to move.

The perceptual system uses more than the information concerning movement of the eyes and passage of images across the retina in deciding what is moving in relation to what. K. Duncker showed that the brain takes account of the size of objects in deciding on relative movement. He shone a spot of light onto a large screen and moved the screen to the right. Most observers reported that they saw the screen as stationary and the spot of light moving to the left: the perceptual system assumes that smaller objects are more likely to move. In this example the perception of movement contradicts the information from the eye and image-movement systems.

Depth/Distance

The real world, like the perceived world, has three dimensions – height, width and depth. The retina, however, is only two-dimensional and this raises the problem of how it is possible to code the relative distance of objects from the observer. Paintings and photographs demonstrate that it is possible to conclude something about depth from the clues contained in two-dimensional representations; the brain uses many of these, such as perspective and relative size – the fact that objects in the distance cause a smaller image on the retina than the same objects at close quarters – to make its decision, but also takes advantage of the fact that we have two eyes. If an object is very far in front of the observer each eye looks almost straight ahead but as the object gets closer the eyes converge. This can be demonstrated by holding a finger in front of a subject and asking him to watch it as you move toward him; the eyes start to converge until at a point about an inch from his nose they are almost crossed.

The angle of convergence of the eyes is one clue that the brain uses to determine depth but on its own it is not enough since it only allows the perception of distance of one object at a time. Each eye receives a slightly different view of the world, as can be seen by looking at a scene through first one eye and then the other. This difference is greater when viewing near rather than far objects and is known as *retinal disparity*. When viewing two objects at four and six feet from the observer, retinal disparity is quite large; but if the observer is thirty feet away from the two objects the disparity will be much less and so the objects will appear closer together. Retinal disparity on its own, therefore, is not enough to give a true perception of relative depth. The perceptual system overcomes this difficulty by combining information from convergence and retinal disparity, so that when the convergence clue indicates that the object is far away, small disparities are considered to indicate larger differences in distance than when the convergence clue indicates that the eyes are focused on objects nearer the eyes.

The Auditory System

There are close parallels between the visual and auditory systems. Sound-waves are alternate compressions and thinnings-out of air, rather like waves in a pond. There are two principal kinds of information carried by sound-waves: *pitch* and *volume*. The pitch of a sound refers to how high the note is: a high note is a high-pitched note. Pitch – or *frequency* – is calculated according to the number of sound-wave peaks which pass a fixed point per second, and is expressed in cycles per second, or Herz.

Volume is determined by the height – or *amplitude* – of a particular sound-wave. Most of the coding of sound involves transducing pitch and volume into electrical impulse form. This is the function of the auditory sense organ, the ear. The ear consists of three main sections, called from the outside inwards – as the names suggest – the *outer ear*, which is exposed to external air; the *middle ear*, which is air-filled but not directly exposed; and the *inner ear*, which is fluid-filled.

Figure 17. Cross-section of the Human Ear

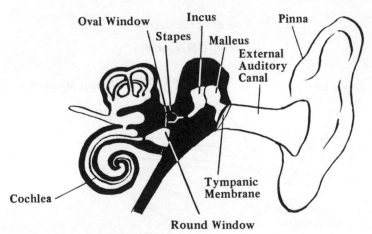

The outer ear incorporates the *pinna* and the *external auditory canal*. The pinna acts as a sound-catcher, but in humans is less effective than the movable pinna of, for example, dogs. At the far end of the outer ear is the *tympanic membrane* or *eardrum* which acts just like the skin of a drum, being beaten by the sound-waves travelling down the external ear canal. The wax in the ear acts as a protective screen for the skin of the ear canal, preventing bacterial infection; it also traps foreign bodies, such as insects, which are ejected with the wax.

Figure 18a. Straightened-out View of Cochlea

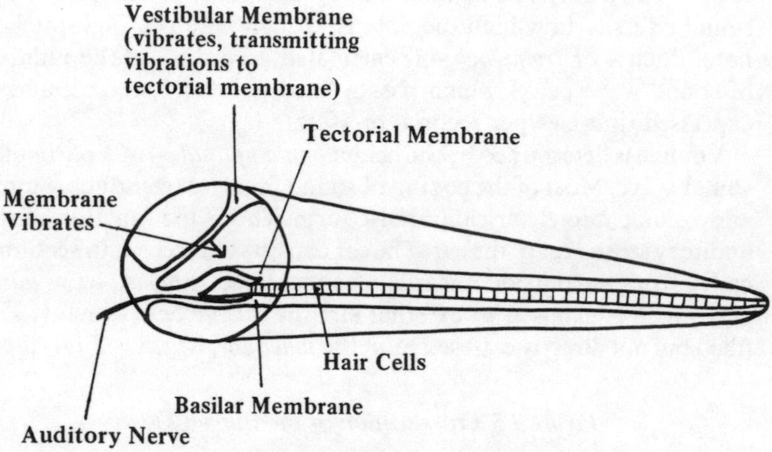

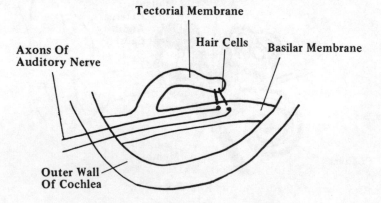

Figure 18b. Enlarged Cross-section of Cochlea

The movement in the eardrum caused by sound waves is very tiny and needs to be amplified. Amplification is the function of the three bones in the middle ear called *ossicles*. The *malleus* or *hammer*, the *incus* or *anvil*, and the *stapes* or *stirrup* therefore act as levers, taking the vibrations from the eardrum and increasing their force. This amplification is necessary because the inner ear is fluid-filled, and more pressure is needed in a sound-wave if it is to pass through fluid.

These more powerful vibrations from the stapes enter the *cochlea* or inner ear via the *fenestra ovalis* or *oval window*. It is here in the cochlea itself that the transduction from pressure-wave to electrical impulse takes place. In figure 18 the snailshell-shaped cochlea has been straightened out, to show its internal structure.

As the pressure-waves make the cochlear fluid vibrate, the *basilar membrane* also vibrates. The *hair cells* which are embedded in the basilar membrane are in contact with the *tectorial membrane*; any movement of the basilar membrane therefore causes the hair cells to be moved. These compressions cause the hair cells to fire. The electrical impulses from each hair cell leave the ear by way of the auditory nerve.

Pitch or Frequency
Notice in figure 18 that hair cells at the outermost end of the cochlea – towards the pinna – are most sensitive to high frequencies of sound, up to 20,000 cycles per second. The hair cells at the opposite end are sensitive to lower frequencies, down to about 1,000 cycles per second. Thus the process of coding pitch becomes evident: hair cells at the pinna end of the cochlea signal high frequency, and at the other end low frequency.

However, for frequencies below about 1,500 cycles per second a different coding system seems to take over. The whole basilar membrane reproduces the particular frequency, for example to register a frequency of 500 cycles per second the basilar membrane also vibrates at 500 cycles per second. Individual groups of hair cells send volleys of impulses down the auditory nerve at that particular frequency.

Once coded, the impulses travel from the cochlea down the auditory nerve to the brain, which then decodes the information. Some groups of hair cells, when they fire, represent high-frequency sound; some medium; and some low. If volleys of impulses come from all hair cells, the frequency at which the impulses arrive gives the frequency of the sound.

Volume or Amplitude

The volume of a sound is conveyed by the rate of firing of hair cells, or more often by the number of cells firing: the more cells firing, the higher the volume of the sound. In addition, some hair cells have predetermined, higher thresholds; for example, a hair cell with a predetermined threshold of 100 units of volume will begin to fire only when the volume reaches 100 units, and not before.

Inside the brain is a cross-over network, very similar to that in visual coding. There is a cross-over of fibres from one cochlea to the opposite hemisphere of the brain. The cross-over is not 'half and half' as in vision; in fact more than half the fibres cross over.

In the auditory cortex – the area of the brain which decodes electrical impulses from the ear – are situated the auditory equivalents of receptive fields. Certain groups of neurons receive impulses from the auditory nerve. Some nerve cells respond only to the beginning of a tone; some decrease their firing rate if a sound continues; and others continue to fire if a tone is continued. Notice again that this is not a full analysis of the processes involved in auditory perception: once the brain has received this coded information, it again has to interpret it, according to previous experiences, interests, and so on.

When you are first learning to speak a foreign language, it is difficult to pick out individual words in a conversation, because the native speaker seems to talk so quickly; but when you have learnt more of the language, you notice that the native speaker no longer seems to be talking so fast, and that you can pick out individual words easily. The change is not in the speaker, but in you, the listener. As a result of your learning of the language, your auditory system becomes able to interpret the same sounds in a different way.

Summary

1 The rods and cones of the retina produce nerve impulses when stimulated by light. In normal light the cones are most active and allow colour vision; the rods are responsible for twilight vision.
2 A visual image causes nerve impulses to pass to the visual cortex via the optic nerve, optic chiasma and lateral geniculate body.
3 Cells in the visual cortex fire when groups of retinal cells known

as receptive fields are stimulated, giving the perceptual system information about shape.

4 Movement of an image across the retina causes sequential firing
of cortical cells with adjacent receptive fields and this may cause the
perception of movement but is interpreted in the light of eye movement. Even when this system signals the movement of one object
rather than another the perceptual system may accept a different
interpretation based on expectation.

5 The separation of the eyes causes them to receive slightly different
views. The extent of this disparity is larger for near than for distant
objects. The eyes converge when they fix on close objects and the
perceptual system combines this together with retinal disparity to
interpret distance. Other clues to distance include perspective and
the fact that the same object at a greater distance causes a smaller
image on the retina.

6 Hearing involves the coding of sound energy in the ear from
sound-waves into electrical energy; this is done in the cochlea, the
inner ear.

7 The cochlea contains hair cells embedded in a flexible membrane,
with their other ends touching a fixed membrane. The fluid in the
cochlea is made to vibrate by the three ear bones (malleus, incus
and stapes) connecting the tympanic membrane and cochlea.

8 Movement of the flexible membrane causes the hair cells to be
compressed, and this compression triggers the electrical impulse
which passes from the cochlear nerve to the auditory cortex.

9 Different areas of the cochlea code different pitches, but below
1500 cycles per second the entire basilar membrane vibrates at the
same rate.

10 Decoding of auditory information is performed in the auditory
cortex, which itself contains auditory receptive fields.

11 Although the findings in this section show how external stimuli
are transduced into electrical impulses and passed to the brain, it
must be remembered that this is only the beginnings of perception:
the individual reorganizes and interprets the information according
to his previous experiences, motivation and emotional states.

Chapter 3

The Basic Mechanisms of Heredity

An individual's life starts at the moment of conception when a sperm from the father fertilizes an egg from the mother. In some animals, such as fish, this process occurs outside the body, the female fish laying eggs onto which the male sheds his sperm; in mammals, and this includes humans, the process occurs within the womb of the female. However, in both cases conception starts a train of events which under normal circumstances leads to the production of another individual of the species. In many ways the new individual will be similar to its parents, but in other ways the youngster will differ in terms of appearance or behaviour. 'Genetics', the scientific study of *heredity*, attempts to analyse and explain these differences and similarities. Heredity, of course, is not the sole factor which influences similarities or differences between you and other people; the environment also has a great effect from conception onwards – your sensory experiences, the physical and social world in which you live, and external events – but it is heredity which lays the foundation on which all these other factors are superimposed. Heredity provides a kind of 'blueprint' which determines the characteristics of the individual; this is contained in the chromosomes, which are present in the nucleus of every cell in your body.

Chromosomes and Genes

The human body is composed of millions of cells; they constitute the different tissues and organs which combine to form the individual. The hereditary details on the *chromosomes* dictate the characteristics of the cell which contains them. Thus, while every nucleus holds all the hereditary information passed from the parents, each cell uses only that part of the blueprint which is necessary for its particular role. This ensures that a cell in one part of the body will perhaps act as a 'building block' for the heart, while one in another part may be a 'building block' for the liver or nervous system. It is as though hereditary information were contained in a large book, of which every cell of the body had a copy open at the page relevant to that cell. However, the 'book' takes the chemical form of thousands of genes which are carried on the string-like chromosomes.

Each species of animal has a characteristic number of chromosomes, which are found in pairs in most animals: man has 23 pairs, rhesus monkeys 24 pairs, goldfish 47 pairs, and shrimps have over 100 pairs. One chromosome from each pair comes from the mother and the other from the father.

The genes are also arranged in pairs. If we look at a pair of chromosomes within a nucleus the genes on one chromosome are responsible for the same attributes in the individual as those on its partner. The determination of a particular characteristic depends on the character of both genes: if both genes governing eye colour are blue-eye genes then the individual will have blue eyes; if both are for brown eyes he will have brown eyes. However, if the gene for one chromosome is for blue eyes and the other for brown eyes the individual will have brown eyes because the brown-eye gene is *dominant*. This brown-eyed individual will still have a gene for blue eyes. Because the blue-eye gene is 'dominated' by the brown, it is given the name *recessive*. This means that we cannot tell simply by observation of an individual which genes are present in his make-up. There is an important distinction between *genotype*, the genetic make-up of an individual, and *phenotype*, the characteristics of the individual as they actually develop. The brown-eyed individual with two brown-eye genes and the browned-eyed individual with one brown- and one blue-eyed gene have similar phenotypes but different genotypes. Conversely two individuals with the same genotype may have different phenotypes, for example when one of a pair of individuals, each possessing the genotype to be tall, suffers from malnutrition and therefore does not grow fully.

Some characteristics like eye colour are determined by single pairs of genes but often many pairs govern the display of more complex characteristics such as intelligence.

The Transmission of Genetic Information from Parents to Children
The human fertilized egg or *zygote* contains twenty-three pairs of

chromosomes, half of which have come from the sperm and half from the egg; the correct number is achieved because the sperm and egg each contain only half the normal number, just one of each pair. The process whereby the cells which produce sperm and eggs divide into two cells containing only twenty-three individual chromosomes is known as *meiosis*. At conception the twenty-three chromosomes of the sperm combine in the same nucleus with those from the egg, re-forming the normal twenty-three pairs each with their own associated genes. Both parents thus contribute equally to the genetic make-up of an individual.

The zygote's development into an embryo and then into the child or offspring involves the repeated division of cells by a process

Figure 19. The Transmission of Genetic Material from Parents to Offspring in an Imaginary Animal with Three Pairs of Chromosomes

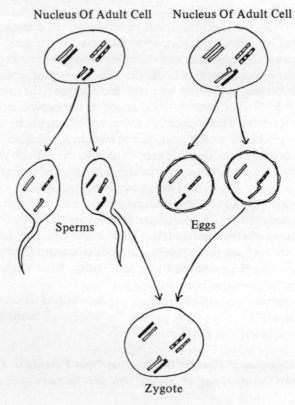

known as *mitosis*; this produces cells each with the constant number of twenty-three pairs of chromosomes.

The two chromosomes in each pair are alike in shape and size except in the twenty-third pair; these are known as the *sex chromosomes* because they determine whether the individual is male or female. In females the sex chromosomes are alike and are called X chromosomes; in males one chromosome is the same as the female chromosome but the other, which is shorter, is known as a Y chromosome. Although the male and the female make an equal contribution to the genetic make-up of the child in the number of chromosomes they pass on, this difference in their sex chromosomes means that the male contribution ultimately determines the sex of the child. This is because egg cells produced by meiosis always contain an X chromosome, but the sperm cells may contain either an X or a Y chromosome; if an X sperm fertilizes the egg the offspring will be female – XX – but if a Y sperm does so the offspring will be male – XY. Because the X chromosome is longer than the Y it can carry extra genes which in females will have corresponding partners on the other X chromosomes. Their effect on the characteristics of the individual will then depend on whether they are dominant or recessive. In the male, of course, they will have no corresponding genes on the shorter Y chromosome and will thus have their effect on the individual's attributes without any necessity for being dominant. This lesser number of genes does not normally disadvantage the male, but *haemophilia* is an exception to this.

Some Genetic Disorders

Haemophilia
Patients suffering from haemophilia are nearly all male. Because their blood does not clot they are in continual danger of bleeding to death; the smallest wound takes a very long time to heal. The condition is caused by an abnormal gene which is recessive and is situated on the X chromosome but not on the shorter Y chromosome; thus if a male has this recessive gene he can have no dominant gene to counteract it. On the other hand a woman with a haemophilia gene on one X chromosome is likely to have the normal and dominant blood-clotting gene on her other X chromosome; however, she may pass on the recessive gene to her children, in which case she is called a 'carrier'.

Because of its association with the X chromosome and its predominance in males, haemophilia is known as a 'sex-linked' disorder. As the gene for haemophilia is carried only on the X chromosome a boy can inherit it only from his mother, for if the child is male the father will have provided a Y chromosome, which will be unaffected. Haemophilia, then, has the strange property of being a disease suffered mainly by males but transmitted only by female

Figure 20. The Inheritance of Haemophilia

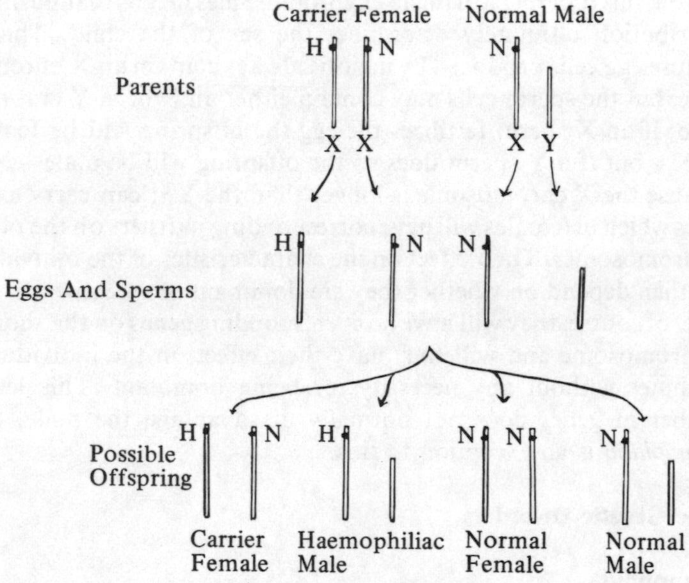

Carrier Female   Normal Male

H   N   N

Parents

X X   X Y

Eggs And Sperms

H   N   N

Possible Offspring

H   N   H   N   N   N

Carrier   Haemophiliac   Normal   Normal
Female   Male   Female   Male

carriers. Queen Victoria was a carrier for haemophilia and through her daughters the gene was introduced into the royal families of Spain and Russia.

Figure 20 shows the variations possible in the types of children produced by a 'normal' father and a carrier mother. It illustrates how both the sperm and the egg contain only one of the sex chromosomes of the parent. There will be equal numbers of female eggs with normal and with haemophiliac genes; the chance of producing a son with the disorder will be one in four.

Phenylketonuria or PKU

Most people have a couple of chromosomes containing the gene pair known as PP, which controls the breakdown of *phenylalanine*, a substance contained in many everyday foods. However, patients suffering from *PKU* have instead a pair of recessive genes, pp, which cause phenylalanine to be only partially broken down into a substance which is poisonous to the nervous system and thus causes mental retardation. Because the abnormal gene p is recessive an individual with the dominent gene P on one chromosome and p on its partner

Figure 21. The Inheritance of PKU from Carrier Parents

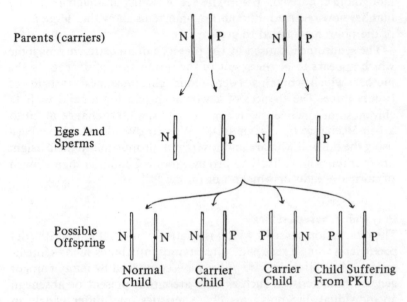

Parents (carriers)	N P	N P	
Eggs And Sperms	N P	N P	
Possible Offspring	N N	N P	P N	P P
	Normal Child	Carrier Child	Carrier Child	Child Suffering From PKU

will appear perfectly normal but will in fact be a carrier who may pass on the gene to his children. If two carriers have children it is likely that some of them will show the disorder, as figure 21 shows.

At present the disease affects about one child in forty thousand born in England. It can be diagnosed by analysis of the child's urine; if it is detected early enough the child may grow up normally by taking a special diet which is free from phenylalanine. This gives us a demonstration of a way in which the development of a hereditary characteristic may be altered by changes in the environment: in the past children with PKU usually died early and the survivors very rarely had children of their own, but with today's screening and treatment techniques they are likely to lead normal lives and become parents. The children of a couple who both have PKU will all inherit the disorder because their parents will have only the recessive gene to pass on to them.

Mongolism

Children suffering from *mongolism*, also known as *Down's syndrome*, have a characteristic slant-eyed, oriental appearance; they are often very affectionate but are always mentally retarded. Most mongoloid children die before the age of twenty although a growing number now reach adulthood. Post-mortems show that large areas of the brain have failed to grow.

The syndrome is caused by the presence of an extra chromosome which appears to be the result of the production of an egg by the mother which contains twenty-four chromosomes, instead of twenty-three. The chances of a woman producing a child with 47 chromosomes increase with age from a 1-in-2,000 chance at 20 to a 1-in-50 chance by the age of 40. Women over 35 who have been using the Pill and who are underweight in proportion to their height are four times more likely to produce mongol children than women of normal weight or women not on the Pill.

Polygenic Characteristics

The retardation caused by PKU is relatively unusual in that it is dependent on a single gene pair, whereas most attributes such as intelligence and emotionality are *polygenic* – controlled by many pairs of genes. Characteristics such as PKU are either present or absent in an individual, but polygenic characteristics may differ widely in degree according to the properties of all the individual genes affecting them. In addition intelligence and emotionality, like PKU, are influenced by environmental factors.

One experiment shows the extent to which emotionality can be affected by heredity. The selective breeding of those animals which show a predominance of either 'emotional' or 'non-emotional' genes demonstrates the possible variations. Rats, for example, differ in their degree of emotionality, hence the disparities between them in their reactions to the open field test. The 'open field' is neither open nor a field: it is an enclosed area in which a rat can be subjected to mildly frightening noise and lights. The floor of the open field is marked off into sections so that the experimenter can record the rat's mobility by counting the number of sections it enters; an emotional rat produces more faeces and moves less under these conditions than a less emotional rat.

In 1960 P. L. Broadhurst showed that heredity was very important in determining the degree of a rat's emotionality. He selected the most emotional rats and allowed them to mate; the most emotional rats from their offspring were then allowed to mate and this was repeated for many generations. He also took the rats showing least emotion and, following the same pattern, allowed them to mate. The young of the emotional rats were much more emotional than those of the less emotional rats even though they were all raised in a very similar environment; this difference increased with successive generations. To ensure that emotionality was not simply learnt from their mothers Broadhurst took half the young of the emotional mothers and had them reared by the less emotional mothers while half the young of the less emotional mothers were reared by emotional mothers. However, he found that the emotionality of the young was still affected by their heredity much more than by the different environmental conditions provided by the mothers.

It is likely that emotionality is controlled by many rather than just one pair of genes; of these more are 'emotional' than 'non-emotional' in emotional rats. When Broadhurst picked out the most emotional of each generation to mate with each other a greater and greater percentage of 'emotional' genes was being passed on to each successive generation.

When Broadhurst mated males from one strain with females of the opposite strain he found that the offspring were of intermediate emotionality.

Genes and Evolution

It was once thought that if a person trained very hard to become an athlete, developing all the muscles in his body, he would pass his new physique on to his children. This idea, known as the 'Lamarckian hypothesis', has been shown to have no basis in fact. The genotype to be tall, in an individual, is not affected if he suffers from malnutrition and thus does not grow fully. Only genetic information is passed on through heredity and the genes themselves cannot be changed by our experiences in life.

However, some genes make an animal better suited to its environment and thus do make it more likely to survive and to pass on its genes to the next generation. One of the most striking examples of evolutionary change of this kind has occurred since the Industrial Revolution in the change of the proportion of dark and light in the colour of peppered moths. More than a century ago the majority of these moths were light in colour, with a few dark individuals. As the trees on which the moths rested tended to be light in colour, birds were more likely to see the dark-coloured moths and eat them; by reducing their numbers the birds prevented them from passing on their dark-colour genes. As more and more smoke poured from factories and trains into the atmosphere the trunks of trees became darker and the original disadvantage of dark colouring was reversed. By 1900 approximately ninety-nine per cent of all peppered moths were dark in colour because they were least often caught by birds and thus survived to pass their genes on to the next generation.

In the case of the peppered moth the genes for darkness were already present in the population, but new genes and new species can arise. New genes may be formed by a process known as *mutation*; this is a change in the chemical composition of a gene that is usually caused by radioactivity or by chemicals. In order to be effective the mutation must occur in the cells which form the eggs or sperms to be passed on to the next generation; this may then show a difference in form or behaviour from its parents. The theory of evolution suggests that all changes that have occurred in the development from simple life-forms to ourselves have been small steps caused by mutations, each of which produced animals more fitted to survive in their environment. It has been calculated that under normal conditions the rate of gene mutation in most animals is about one in half-a-million genes at each place on the chromosomes in each generation; such figures explain why evolution is such a slow process. Although normal levels of radiation, such as that from sunlight, produce this low level of mutations, a nuclear bomb or leak from a nuclear power station would produce many more; most of these mutations would probably produce offspring incapable of survival while others might produce offspring with abnormalities such as lack of limbs or mental retardation. A very small proportion of such mutations might prove to have beneficial effects, but none have yet been observed.

Summary

1 Twenty-three pairs of chromosomes are contained in the nucleus of all normal human cells except in those of the sperm and eggs, which contain twenty-three individual chromosomes. One pair of chromosomes determines the sex of the individual.

2 Each chromosome contains many genes which control the activity of the cells and hence have an effect on the physical and psychological characteristics of the individual. Most characteristics are governed by more than one pair of genes. Some genes are dominant, some recessive.

3 Individuals obtain an equal number of chromosomes from each parent. The sex of the individual depends on whether the egg is fertilized by a sperm containing an X or a Y chromosome.

4 Patients suffering from haemophilia continue to bleed after being cut because their blood does not clot. Although nearly all sufferers are male, the disorder is passed on from the mother because it is controlled by a recessive gene on the X chromosome.

5 PKU is a genetic disorder caused by the presence of a pair of recessive genes which cannot control the breakdown of phenylalanine. The disorder leads to mental retardation but this may be prevented by the adoption of a phenylalanine-free diet early in life.

6 Mongolism is caused by the presence at conception of an extra chromosome.

7 Broadhurst showed that hereditary factors are very important in the determination of the degree of a rat's emotionality. Emotionality is a polygenic characteristic and selective breeding can produce rats of very high or very low emotionality.

8 Gene mutation has caused animals to evolve. Those animals with genes that fit them for survival in a particular situation reproduce and continue their species in that environment whereas others become extinct. In normal circumstances genes are rarely affected by the process of mutation, but when this process is speeded up by the action of nuclear radiation the effects may be disastrous.

Chapter 4

The Nature/Nurture Debate on Perception

First, a few terms should be explained. *Perception* is not the same as *seeing*. In psychology, 'seeing' is simply the physical process in which patterns of light fall on the retina, the light-sensitive area at the back of the eye. Another word more often used instead of 'seeing' is *sensation*, or sensory information. 'Perception', on the other hand, is defined as the organization and translation of sensations by the brain.

The question we shall be investigating in this chapter will be: does our ability to organize and translate our sensory information have to be learnt – acquired by nurture – or is it built into us even before birth – acquired through nature? This is the heart of the nature/nurture debate on perception – whether our perceptual abilities are *innate*, i.e. developed before birth, or learnt.

The nature/nurture debate has arisen because there is both evidence which suggests that some parts of perception may be innate and evidence which indicates that other parts have to be learnt. There are thus two main groups or schools of psychologists who debate the matter.

The Nurture School

The members of this school are also called *learning theorists* or *empiricists*, of whom the main exponent is the Canadian psychologist, D. O. Hebb. The empiricists believe that although the simplest form of perception, *figure/ground* – the ability to perceive that there is 'something there', standing out from the background – is probably innate, all the rest of our perceptual abilities have to be learnt or are determined by our environment. Hebb's belief is that our experiences cause changes in the cells which actually make up the perceptual system: cells begin to link together, and to work as groups which are known as *cell assemblies*; they become organized, and begin to organize the information they receive.

William James, one of the early empiricists, wrote that the new-born baby's world was 'one blooming, buzzing confusion'. By this he meant that although the baby's senses were receiving all the sensory information, it was unable to organize and translate this information into successful perception. Babies can therefore see but cannot perceive.

The Nature School

The members of this school are called *innate theorists* or *nativists*. The main exponents are the *Gestaltists*, who believe that most of our perceptual abilities are present at birth. The Gestalt school arose in direct opposition to William James's ideas. The word 'Gestalt' is German, and means shape or form. Whereas James believed that we learn to perceive by building up our perceptions with the pieces provided by experience, the Gestaltists argued that we just perceive a shape, a Gestalt, whole and complete.

The next problem which arises is how to determine which of these opposing theories is correct, or whether both of them have some validity. We cannot ask a baby to tell us what it perceives, but fortunately there are several ways of overcoming this difficulty. An examination of the evidence from various types of investigation will demonstrate the balance of support for the two schools of thought.

Deprivation Studies   Nurture

Humans
If an adult who has been blind all his life is suddenly given his sight, he will be and behave, as far as perception is concerned, as an 'adult new-born'. This has the advantage for psychologists that he can take part in relatively complicated experiments and – unlike a baby – report his experiences verbally. One of the best-known investigations of this type is that described in 1963 by R.L. Gregory. What seems to happen is that the person can at first see only the figure/ground phenomenon: he is aware that there is something standing out against a background but remains unable to recognize it by sight alone. If he has handled objects before losing his sight, however,

he is able to perceive them much more clearly. This ability to use information from one sense to assist a different sense is known as *cross-modal transfer*. After a fairly short period of time the subject is generally able to overcome the initial problems and to perceive fairly normally. Gregory quotes these findings to suggest that perception is largely learnt.

However, not much reliance can be placed on these studies for the following reasons:

1 Adults gaining sight are not the same as babies, whose visual systems may still be maturing: they have other senses which are already well developed to give them clues – taste, touch, hearing and smell.

2 Cases of adults learning to perceive have been few in number, and inadequately reported. Usually little care was taken to note down or verify the patients' experiences.

3 Adults' previous learning may actually interfere with the new perceptual learning, because people tend to find it easier to use the system they already know than the one they do not. Thus Gregory's subject continued to prefer touch to vision.

4 Most subjects are unprepared for the new visual world with which they are confronted: they are frightened and depressed by it. Gregory's patient in fact died, at least partially of depression, about three years after he gained his sight. Such emotional disturbances may affect the way in which subjects perceive, thus making them unsuitable for study.

Animals

In 1947 A. N. Riesen kept a group of chimpanzees in darkness from birth until they had matured, and compared their perceptual abilities with those of normally reared chimpanzees. The group deprived of light showed markedly inferior perceptual abilities. However, it has since been discovered by L. Weiscrantz that the retinas of the chimps reared in darkness had not developed properly and contained fewer retinal cells. Riesen's experiment may therefore show only that light is physically necessary to maintain the visual system or to help it mature.

Riesen next attempted to allow for this possibility in his experiments by testing chimps which had been raised wearing translucent goggles, which allow only diffused, non-imaged light – light which contains no pictures – to enter the eye. He still found that these chimps had markedly inferior vision to those raised in a normal environment. If perception is innate the young chimps' environment should of course have had no effect on their perception; that the environment did have effects therefore suggests that the perceptual system can be modified by experience and, as suggested by human deprivation studies, by learning.

Further support for this view comes from D. H. Hubel and T. N. Wiesel who found in 1963 that kittens reared in translucent goggles did not develop normal arrangements of receptive fields on the retina. (Receptive fields, it will be remembered, are groups of perhaps several thousand retinal cells, each of which registers a line at a specific angle belonging to the image before the eye; they then transmit their information to the brain.)

Similarly, in 1966 C. Blakemore and G. F. Cooper brought up cats in a 'vertical world', in a drum which had only vertical lines drawn on it. The cats were therefore presented with images, but these were very specific, being vertical only. When the cats had matured their perceptual abilities were tested, and it was found that they were unable to perceive horizontal lines. Their receptive fields had developed, but only those which registered vertical lines would operate: horizontal lines had no effect on them. However, this does not necessarily prove that line recognition has to be learnt: it may be that receptive fields capable of registering lines at all angles are present at birth but that unused fields deteriorate, or are 'taken over' by fields registering vertical lines.

Thus it seems that the type of environment is important in the development of perception; this in turn suggests that learning plays at least some part in perception, and that it is not all innate. However, visual experience alone is not enough. R. Held and A. Hein, for example, showed that for perceptual development to take place fully the tested subject must be allowed to use its eyes and also to manipulate, or at least move around in, its environment. In figure 22 both kittens, A and B, are given exactly the same amount of visual experience and exactly the same type of experience. Kitten A's movements are transmitted via a system of pulleys to kitten B's basket so that any movements made by kitten A are transmitted automatically to kitten B. Thus both kittens have exactly the same amount of movement in their environment, the only difference being that kitten A's movements are active – it moves by itself – and kitten B's are passive: its movements are controlled by kitten A.

Figure 22. The 'Kitten Carousel' (Held and Hein's Experiment)

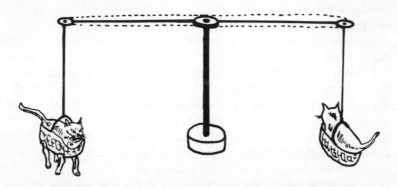

Because both kittens had exactly the same amounts and types of visual experience, any differences in their perceptual abilities should have been caused by their active/passive roles. The passive kitten in fact showed much less perceptual development than the active kitten, which suggests that activity in or interaction with the environment is necessary for full perceptual development.

To summarize the significant findings of deprivation studies: both patterned (imaged) visual experience and the ability to interact with the environment appear to be necessary for the development of normal perceptual abilities.

Distortion or Readjustment Studies

The aim of this type of study is to determine whether adults can adjust to a new visual environment. If it can be shown that adults' perceptual systems are flexible and can exhibit signs of having developed by learning then it is possible that the new-born – *neonate* – also possess a flexible perceptual system which is shaped by learning: an innate perceptual system would presumably be inflexible and incapable of being shaped.

Lower animals – lizards, frogs and chickens, for example – do not appear able to adjust to a distorted visual world: chickens wearing goggles that distort their vision by 10° to the right never adapt enough to compensate for the distortion and miss the grain at which they are pecking by 10° each time (E. H. Hess, 1963).

However, studies of adult humans wearing distorting goggles have shown that humans have a much greater ability to adapt to a changed

Nature
as chicken
couldn't
adapt

visual world. Ivo Kohler wore goggles in which the left half of each
lens was red and the right half green. At first his visual world
appeared red when he looked to the left and green when he looked
to the right. After only a few hours this apparent division was no
longer experienced: he had evidently adjusted to compensate for the
change. However, when he removed the goggles, Kohler found that
his visual world seemed to be coloured in the opposite direction to
that experienced when wearing goggles, but only for a short time,
after which it returned to normal. Once more he had been able to
adjust. Kohler also experimented on himself and others using
goggles which inverted or displaced objects in their visual world. At
first he experienced great disorientation and nausea but after several
days was able to adjust and live reasonably normally.

   G. M. Stratton performed similar experiments on himself using in-
verting goggles. After a few days' adaptation he was able to move
around normally and his visual world appeared to be the right way
up except when he really concentrated. On removal of the goggles
there was again a reversed after-effect, which lasted only a short time.

   Such evidence from readjustment studies seems to show that perception is learnt, because a totally innate perceptual system would
tend to remain inflexible. However, there is a difficulty here and one
which crops up often in psychology. Because an adult is able to learn
to perceive his world in a different way, we must not automatically
assume that a child originally has to learn to perceive. The readjustment studies do not finally resolve the nature/nurture debate.

Behavioural Studies of the Neonate or New-Born

We cannot ask babies how they perceive, but we can often tell when
they are frightened, for they cry, and when they are happy, because
they laugh. Babies do not use words to communicate but gestures:
their behaviour – the actions they perform – tells us. Behavioural
studies of the neonate therefore infer perceptual processes from the
behaviour of offspring. For example, if a baby could perceive something which was frightening, it would tend to back away from it;
if we show a frightening object to the baby and it does back away,
we can thus infer that it has been able to perceive it.

   The most famous of the behavioural neonate studies is possibly
that of E. J. Gibson and R. D. Walk in 1960. Babies often fall down
steps and it had previously been argued that they learn to perceive
depth from these painful experiences. However, Gibson and Walk's

work seems to show that this is not the case. They constructed an apparatus known as the 'visual cliff' (see figure 23). Towards one end of the apparatus, immediately under the glass 'floor', was stuck some black-and-white checkered material; towards the other, the material was placed about four feet below the glass. The effect was therefore that of a visual cliff on the right-hand side of the apparatus in the figure.

The baby was placed on the central plank and its mother called to it alternately from the 'deep' and 'shallow' sides. The infants used as subjects, who were aged between six and fourteen months, would crawl to their mothers over the 'shallow' side, but would not move over the 'deep' side. Occasionally babies would fall onto the glass

Figure 23. The 'Visual Cliff' (Gibson and Walk's Experiment)

Shallow Side   Baby   Deep Side

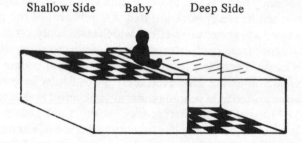

over the 'deep' side; they would then show no fear until they looked down. They were obviously relying on visual information to such an extent that it overrode touch information. It seems then that if infants of this age fall down steps and off chairs it is not because they do not see the depth but because they have yet to develop adequate control of their movements.

Other animals tested on the visual cliff all similarly demonstrated an ability to judge depth. Day-old chicks never strayed onto the 'deep' side; lambs and kids placed on the 'deep' side refused to stand; and kittens either froze or circled backwards aimlessly. Rats, however, based their depth perception more on touch than vision, and showed no preference for either the 'deep' or the 'shallow' side. When their whiskers – their main touch-sensors – were trimmed, they were forced to use vision, and also refused to move onto the deep side.

Gibson and Walk suggest that the main way in which depth is detected in this experiment is through *motion parallax*: when we move our heads from side to side, distant or deep objects appear to move less than near objects; hence the moon will appear to us to keep pace with a car in which we are travelling. These results suggest, but still do not prove, that depth perception is innate in humans: the babies were aged between six and fourteen months, and may have been able to learn depth perception during that time.

There are several experiments which show that babies can distinguish different patterns and that they prefer some patterns to others. In 1966, R.L. Fantz found that a bull's-eye pattern was preferred to stripes, checks and geometrical shapes, and that a drawing of

Figure 24. Face Shapes of the Type Used in Fantz's Experiment

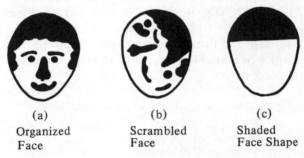

(a)	(b)	(c)
Organized	Scrambled	Shaded
Face	Face	Face Shape

a human face was preferred to all these patterns, and to a jumbled-up drawing of a face. Babies aged between one and fifteen weeks prefer to look at relatively complicated patterns; they are perhaps innately 'programmed' to look at face-like patterns more. However, this experiment (see figure 24) has been criticized, because the human face was more complicated than the geometrical patterns, and the babies may have preferred the complexity to the 'meaning' of the pictures. The babies still preferred the organized to the scrambled face, though there is the possibility that this was more evident in the older neonates than in the younger.

The size and shape *constancies* are the result of perceptual processes which enable us to judge correctly the size and shape of objects no matter how close or how far away they are. An elephant on the horizon still looks big, and an ant close to our feet still looks small; however, the images of them both on the retina may actually be the same size. With an object's increasing distance its image size decreases, but size constancy enables us to overcome this false information from the retina, and to realize that the elephant is not really as small as the ant but is just much further away. Some investigations by T.G. Bower in 1967 gave some indications about whether size constancy is innate or learnt. An empiricist would argue that an infant would respond to the size and shape of objects as these images appeared to his eyes and would not show perceptual constancy, because he would not yet have had time to learn it. A nativist, on the other hand, would argue that because perception is innate the infant should show perceptual constancy.

In figure 25 the two-week-old baby is placed on the table in a comfortable cot from which he can see an object. He comes to learn that if he turns his head to one side he is rewarded by an adult playing peek-a-boo and tickling him. This is called *Operant Conditioning* (see page 77). Once the baby is conditioned to pay attention to the stimulus object in this way the stimulus can be changed, and the baby's head-turns can then be used as a measure of how similar he considers any new stimulus object is to the one he had been conditioned to look at.

Figure 25. General Layout of Bower's Experiment

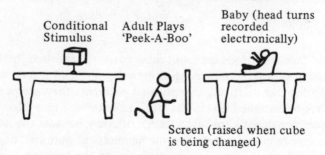

Using the different-sized cubes shown in figure 26 placed at their stated distances, Bower found that the infant responded most to the cube of the same size even when it was moved further away than it had been during the conditioning trials; next most preferred was the cube which was the same distance away as the original cube but a different size; and the least preferred was that which was a different size and at a different distance, even though this projected the same retinal image as the original object.

The fact that the baby was able to recognize the original cube at a different distance suggests that it had some form of depth/distance perception and size constancy. If the empiricist view had been correct the baby in the experiment should have chosen the 90-centimetre cube at 3 metres, which gives the same retinal image as the original cube; that it did not, therefore gives strong support to the nativist approach.

Figure 26. Cubes Used in Bower's Experiment

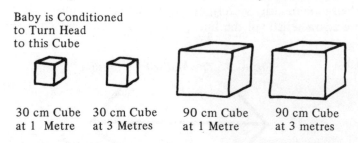

Baby is Conditioned
to Turn Head
to this Cube

| 30 cm Cube | 30 cm Cube | 90 cm Cube | 90 cm Cube |
| at 1 Metre | at 3 Metres | at 1 Metre | at 3 metres |

Empiricists would predict the following order of preference for the test stimuli in figure 26: most preferred would be stimulus 3; next preferred would be stimulus 2; and least preferred would be stimulus 1. Nativists, however, would predict that the reverse should happen and that the preferred order would be 1 most; then 2; and 3 least. In fact, the nativist predictions were firmly upheld by the results of this experiment, suggesting that the baby already had size constancy.

Cross-Cultural Studies
If, for the moment, we accept the empiricist view that perception is learnt it follows that different cultures, which offer different environments, should perhaps provide different forms of perceptual learning. One of the best-known visual illusions, the *Muller–Lyer illusion*, has therefore been used to investigate the nature/nurture debate across several cultures.

The reason why the illusion in figure 27 is produced is this: information reaching our eyes contains *depth cues* – clues which indicate how deep or far away an object is. These depth cues stimulate the size constancy 'programme' in our brains: the further away the object appears, according to the depth cues we receive, the more size constancy is needed and the more applied. Figure 27 quite simply contains false depth cues: the lower object deceives the brain into believing that it is further away than it actually is. Thus the size constancy 'programme' is nevertheless stimulated by these false depth cues and 'expands' the size of the lower figure an unnecessary amount to compensate for distance.

In 1963 M.H. Segall and D.T. Campbell presented the Muller–Lyer illusion to Zulus and, with a simple adaptation, were able to measure the amount by which the lower arrow was 'lengthened'. They found that the Zulus were less susceptible than Europeans to the illusion and put forward the hypothesis that this was because of their unfamiliarity with right-angles and straight lines, which are more characteristic of the European 'carpentered' environment.

Figure 27. The Muller-Lyer Illusion

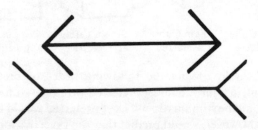

However, later studies by G. Jahoda in 1966 and A.J. Gregor and D.A. McPherson in 1965 have shown that this 'carpentered' environment is not as important as was previously thought. Jahoda argues that Segall's findings were probably influenced by the inability of some racial groups to interpret two-dimensional drawings.

In 1962 M.D. Vernon suggested that differences between individuals and racial groups, in the extent to which they perceive such illusions, may be affected by their varying capacities for size constancy. Artists, for example, are trained to analyse their visual world and do show less size constancy than non-artists, so that they are less affected by the illusion.

In 1932 R. Thouless showed that artists are less affected by size constancy than non-artists and that Indians, who have different artistic methods, are more affected.

In 1957 J.A. Ardis and E. Fraser claimed that personality differences between people affect their susceptibility to size constancy and the illusions but suggested that these differences might be influenced more by the attitude of the subject – either critical or un-critical – than by perceptual organization itself.

In 1962 H.A. Witkin measured how much people from different cultures relied on vision to ascertain their orientation, in other words to ascertain whether or not they were completely upright. His experiments seemed to show that African cultures are less dependent on vision – 'visual field independent' – than Europeans, who are 'visual field dependent'. Africans appear to attach more importance to hearing than Europeans, and to the senses of muscle position and balance.

The existence of these differences, both cross-cultural ones and those produced by training, does demonstrate the significant influence of learning and experience on perception, but it does not prove that all perception has to be learnt.

Conclusions

None of the experiments outlined above proves that all perception is learnt or that it is all innate. However, some general conclusions can be drawn. Deprivation, readjustment and cross-cultural studies suggest that the development of perception is greatly influenced by the environment. Neonate studies, however, show that the young have well developed perceptual systems, including the abilities of depth/distance perception and size and shape constancy.

Early experimenters tried to compare the working of the perceptual system to that of the camera but then found great difficulty in comparing depth-distance perception in the two. J.J. Gibson proposes that this is because a human or animal can move while a camera cannot, so that humans can use motion parallax as a depth cue.

As a result of his experiments Bower stated that the nature/nurture debate is a non-question, because it is based on the false premise that our perceptions are caused by single, fixed retinal images rather like still photographs. Instead, says Bower, our retinal information varies over time: it is a whole series or sequence of images. Babies do not respond to photographs of objects, nor do they respond to retinal images identical to the conditioned stimulus. Therefore Bower suggests that the ability to register the information contained in a static retinal image may be a sophisticated attainment and may have to be learnt, whereas the abilities that the babies showed –

motion parallax, depth perception and the constancies – may well be innate. The major differences between the neonate and the adult perceptual systems, according to Bower, is that the adult's ability to process large quantities of visual information is greater than the neonate's and that the adult also has a greater ability to analyse the retinal image.

Perception and Maturation

Still another factor which confuses the issue is that of maturation. The human infant is born with certain perceptual abilities which develop and decline during his life. This development is influenced not only by learning, as we have suggested, but also by stimulation and maturation. Thus research has shown that general stimulation of an individual produces an increase in brain size, in the number of neural connectors and in learning ability (Rosenzweig, 1971). Also, certainly in animals and probably in humans, maturation affects the organism's ability to obtain stimulation, and conversely stimulation can encourage further maturation processes.

Maturation can be defined as a genetically determined sequence of development. But the fact that it is genetically determined does not mean that it is fixed and inflexible. It can be affected by environmental factors: consider the results of the experiments by Riesen, Blakemore and Cooper, and Held and Hein, on pages 54–6. The empiricists would argue that their findings prove perception to be largely determined by the environment, but this is not really the case. If perception is instead regarded as an ability which matures rather than one which is mainly learnt, or even mainly innate, this would account for the following two observations:

1 Certain structures and abilities may be present at birth but because of lack of use they may atrophy. This may be what happened in some of the experiments mentioned previously.

2 Maturation, as we have said, is a genetically determined sequence of development. However, the fact that a characteristic or ability is genetically 'programmed' does not mean that it must be evident at birth. The ability to walk, for example, depends on maturation, and is not practised at birth. Similarly, therefore, certain perceptual systems may be largely genetically determined and yet may not be in evidence at birth but may also develop later. The impression that they are learnt may thus seem conclusive in some of the findings described and yet is not necessarily so.

The concept of maturation thus provides a half-way house in the debate about innate and environmental factors, and illuminates the ways in which these factors interact: it is actually possible for perception to be both environmentally and innately determined.

In the nature/nurture debate on intelligence which will be examined later, certain psychologists have tried to find out which of the two factors – accepting that both play a part – is the more important. The same attempts cannot really be made for perception, but some clues may be found by looking at the *phylogenesis* of perception. 'Phylogenesis' means the way an ability develops within a species. It appears that the further down the evolutionary scale an animal is the more of its perceptual abilities are innate. Thus certain species of frogs have genetically determined perceptual systems which, without any need for learning, make them very sensitive to images of moving flies, which are their food, projected onto their retinas. If such a frog were surrounded by dead flies it would starve to death because its innate, inflexible perceptual system would not be sensitive to still flies but only to moving ones.

Similarly cuckoos, which are fairly primitive birds, apparently have an innate recognition system for their own species: because the cuckoo lays eggs in the nests of other birds, the young cuckoo, when it hatches, must be provided with an image of its own species so that it can be recognized in the mating season.

Further up the evolutionary scale some species of duck, while not equipped with an innate image of their own species, do have an ability – which may be innate – to learn what their own species looks like; thus they follow and imprint on the first moving object they see (see page 129).

It has been argued that a similar process occurs in humans, but if it does it is nowhere as clearly innate as in ducks: the higher an animal is on the evolutionary scale, the less its perceptual abilities appear to be innately determined.

Summary

1 The nature/nurture debate tries to solve the question of whether our perceptual abilities – or which abilities or processes – are innate or are influenced by our experience with the environment. The former view is termed nativist and the latter empiricist.
2 Deprivation studies, in which an individual is reared without being

allowed to practise normal perception, suggest that the environment does play an important part in the development of perception. However, most of these studies can be criticized because an ability may be innate but may deteriorate through lack of use or may only develop later and therefore appear to be learnt.

3 Distortion studies, which show that an adult can readjust and learn to perceive the world accurately again after his vision has been distorted, suggest perception may be learnt. But the fact that adults can learn to perceive does not prove that babies have to learn.

4 Studies of babies' perceptual abilities – neonate studies – tend to support the nativist view, particularly in experiments with depth/distance perception and size and shape constancy.

5 Cross-cultural studies tend to support the empiricist view because if perception were totally innate different environments should not affect humans' perceptual abilities while these surveys do suggest that different cultures have differences in their perceptual abilities.

6 It may be that the physiological systems involved in perception are genetically determined but that the environment is important in directing how they are used. The concepts of maturation and the phenomenon of imprinting suggest how genetic and environmental factors may actually interact in the development of perception.

Chapter 5

The Development of Learning

In the last chapter attempts were made to determine whether perceptual abilities are innate or whether they have to be learnt. In this chapter we shall look at the best-known forms of learning, but first two fundamental questions must be answered: what does *learning* actually mean, and what happens inside the brain when we learn?

What is Learning?

If you consider the many different kinds of behaviour which are commonly termed learning, you will see that if any definition of learning is to include them all it must be fairly vague. Compare 'learning to perceive' and 'learning psychology for an exam'; the latter involves concentration, application, dedication and frustration, but with the former it is quite unnecessary and inappropriate to sit down and study from books the principles of perception. However, we use the word 'learning' in both cases.

In psychology the most often-used definition is that learning is a relatively permanent change in behaviour as a result of experience; this does not include changes in behaviour brought about by physical damage, disease, drugs or maturation processes. Learning involves changes of behaviour, and presumably because this change of behaviour is relatively permanent, there must also be a relatively permanent change somewhere inside us which allows us, once we have learnt something, to demonstrate this learning again later.

In a book called *The Organization of Behaviour* (John Wiley and Sons, 1949) D.O. Hebb puts forward a theory about the way in which learning occurs and is stored in the brain. At the time of its publication there was very little evidence for this theory because the sophisticated surgical techniques and equipment required to study the functioning of the brain were not yet in existence. As brain researchers have gained more information about the workings of the brain, however, evidence has been mounting that Hebb's theory, although probably not correct in every respect, does seem to have general validity.

Cell Assemblies and Phase Sequences

The essence of Hebb's theory is that the more often two or more brain neurons are made to fire at the same time the greater will be their tendency to act together in the future. Neurons, it will be remembered, can activate each other at the synaptic cleft; the impulse from one neuron can jump this gap in the form of transmitter substances, which then release the impulse from the next neuron in the chain (see figure 4, chapter 1). Two individual neurons which connect via a synaptic cleft may not necessarily be working together because each may be a member of a different circuit in the brain. You can see from figure 28a that the surface area of the synapse is not very large; the bond between the two cells is therefore not very strong. However, according to Hebb's theory, if both these cells fire

Figure 28a. The Synapse Before Learning

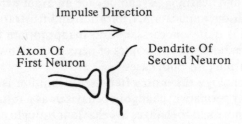

Impulse Direction

Axon Of
First Neuron

Dendrite Of
Second Neuron

Figure 28b. The Synapse After Learning

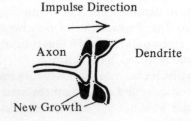

Impulse Direction

Axon   Dendrite

New Growth

at the same time repeatedly we can expect them to be increasingly likely to fire together in future. If the cells are also more strongly joined together physically in the process then they will tend to act as a pair. The place at which this conjunction can occur is the synapse.

Figure 28b shows how the originally weak bond between the cells has become strengthened as the surface areas of the cells on both sides of the synaptic cleft have increased. This increasing amount of substance may thus be the 'raw material' of learning. For the sake of simplicity the strengthening of the bond between only two neurons has been described, but the same process can occur between thousands more.

Hebb's theory was initially based on studies of shape perception; he said that if for example the shape in figure 29 appeared on the

Figure 29. Hebb's Theory of Shape Recognition in Perception

retina it would eventually make certain nerve cells – presumably in the visual cortex – fire. Suppose individual cells in the visual cortex can each register one of the lines in figure 29; where simple cortical cells represent lines, obviously all these cells will fire if the letter A is displayed on the retina. The more often it is displayed, the more likely the cells are to work as a unit in future; the cells capable of representing the various lines will either join together directly or other neurons will assume the role of links between the various cells to form the new cell assembly. This can work as a whole in future to enable recognition of the same shape in different orientations or when parts of it are missing; in other words, we should say we have learnt to recognize the figure and accomplished a kind of learning.

Similarly if we consider the individual cells described as representing not pictorial information in the form of lines but semantic information instead, the meanings of words and perhaps the sounds of the words themselves, we could again apply Hebb's principles, for example to the learning of a poem:

> There was a Canadian named Don
> Whose learning power seemed almost none,
> But he fired a nerve cell
> Which connected like hell –
> Now he's passed his O levels in one.

All the words in the above poem will be familiar to you but their organization into this particular order will be new. This means that you probably already have cell assemblies or *phase sequences*, which are groups of cell assemblies, containing these individual words in your brain. If you wanted to learn this poem off by heart so that you could repeat it correctly what would this task involve as far as the brain is concerned? If the cell assemblies for the individual words already existed, the actual learning task might entail forming new links between these assemblies to create a phase sequence which would contain the words in the necessary order and relationship to one another.

The evidence of a system similar to this was proposed in 1971 by J.R. Anderson and G.H. Bower who were considering the formation of memories which enable the brain to store and retrieve information; their experiments seemed to suggest that learning is often concerned with forming new links between the separate pieces of information already stored in the brain. They called this system of learning *Human Associative Memory* and, although they do not outline a physiological basis for it, it bears a striking resemblance to Hebb's cell-assembly and phase-sequence model.

Hebb's theory, then, describes a possible means by which learning can actually take place in the brain – the linking together of individual neurons to form cell assemblies and of cell assemblies to form phase sequences, which can register increasingly complex information. The following sections cover the theories that are concerned with learning in its more 'external' and readily apparent aspects, but it is essential to realize that these theories, though very different, are all compatible with the ideas about the 'internal' mechanisms of learning described here.

Conditioning

Earlier, learning was defined as a relatively permanent change in behaviour as a result of experience: as a result of having learnt, an animal or person becomes able to demonstrate some kind of behaviour which it could not demonstrate previously. In this section we shall begin by describing some of the simpler forms of learning and then go on to more complex kinds. One of the earliest and most famous theories of learning is called *Classical Conditioning* which is now linked with the name of Ivan Pavlov. In fact he was not the first to devise the technique; an American named Twitmeyer published the results of classical conditioning-type experiments several years before Pavlov but it is Pavlov's name which has become so associated with Classical Conditioning that it is now sometimes known as *Pavlovian Conditioning*; occasionally it is referred to as *Respondent Conditioning*.

Classical Conditioning

Pavlov was a physiologist, working on the salivary reflex in dogs. As part of his experiments he devised an apparatus for measuring the amount of saliva secreted by a dog. Then he noticed that whenever the dog caught sight of the laboratory assistant carrying the pail which contained its food the rate of its salivation increased, even when the dog could not actually see the food inside the pail. Dogs normally salivate only at the sight, smell or taste of food, yet the dog was definitely salivating at the sight of a pail. Pavlov wanted to know why this dog should show such a change from its normal behaviour. He wondered whether, if the dog could associate the pail with its food, it could also associate some completely different object or event with the food and begin to salivate in response to that.

For the next few feedings, each time the dog received its food a bell was sounded for a few seconds, and the amount of saliva secreted was measured. After several such trials Pavlov sounded the bell without the accompaniment of food and the dog still salivated, nearly as much as it normally did when food was presented.

Pavlov gave scientific names to the parts of this procedure. The food is termed the *Unconditional Stimulus* or UCS: it is the stimulus which normally elicits the salivary reflex response. It is 'unconditional' because it works by itself; it needs no other help, or 'conditions', to allow it to work. The bell is a *Conditional Stimulus* or CS because it will only activate the reflex on condition that it is presented at the same time as the food. Salivation to the food is therefore the *Unconditional Response* or UCR: it is a response to an Unconditional Stimulus; and salivation to the bell is a *Conditional Response* or CR – a response to a Conditional Stimulus.

We can summarize Pavlov's procedure in this formula:

The Classical Conditioning Formula

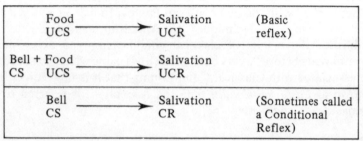

Food UCS	→	Salivation UCR	(Basic reflex)
Bell + Food CS UCS	→	Salivation UCR	
Bell CS	→	Salivation CR	(Sometimes called a Conditional Reflex)

Dogs learn to salivate when they hear the sound of a bell alone, after hearing the bell rung at the same time as they have received food, which does make them salivate. Thus the salivation of a dog to the sound of a bell is conditional upon the bell having been associated with food. Please note that we have used the terms 'unconditional' and 'conditional' here. In some books, you may see the terms 'unconditioned' or 'conditioned' used instead. However, both sets of terms mean the same thing. The use of both endings – 'al' and 'ed' – arose from an error when Pavlov's work was first translated from the original Russian into English. Pavlov actually wrote 'conditional', but this was mistranslated as 'conditioned'.

Extinction of the CR

The UCS *reinforces* the response to the CS: it strengthens it. Without the UCS the CR would not develop. If we now continue to sound the bell but never reinforce the response of the animal with food, the UCS, the CR – salivation – will gradually die out, a process known as *extinction*. If the CS is again rung after a time lapse to give the animal time to rest, the CR may reappear, although it will be much weaker in form. This is known as spontaneous recovery.

Generalization

The basic conditioning process can be made more flexible by *general-ization* Other stimuli, if they are fairly similar to the original CS, will also be found to elicit the response; a bell with a slightly higher or lower tone than the original, for example, or a tapping noise, will probably elicit the salivary response in the experiment just outlined. In effect the animal is able to generalize its behaviour to respond to different stimuli.

Discrimination

The animal can be taught to 'choose' between stimuli, to *discriminate*; for example, we can condition animals to choose specific shapes. If we pair a circular shape with the presentation of food, the animal becomes conditioned to salivate at the appearance of the circle. However, it may, and usually does, generalize the response so that, although a white circle may have been presented originally, the animal will also respond to circles of other colours. In this case we can get the animal to discriminate between these circles, to choose only the white one. This is achieved by reinforcing only the presentation of the white-circle stimulus; because the appearance of differently coloured circles is not reinforced, salivation at their presentation soon stops.

Discrimination is often used for experiments assessing perception in animals. If we want to see whether an animal can perceive a triangle among several other shapes, we condition the animal to salivate at the presentation of a triangle and eliminate any tendency towards generalization so that the animal responds to triangles only. Then the triangle, together with other shapes, is presented to the animal. If it salivates only on the presentation of the triangle we can conclude that the animal has been able to discriminate between the various shapes.

The Use of Classical Conditioning

One way in which Classical Conditioning is being used today is in the area of the treatment of behaviour problems termed 'behaviour therapy'. Behaviour therapists are usually psychiatrists who believe that so-called 'abnormal' behaviour is really a learning problem: the patient may either have failed to learn a particular kind of 'normal' behaviour, or have learnt some kind of 'abnormal' behaviour. Such problems can therefore be treated by conditioning techniques.

One such technique, which is really a standard Classical Conditioning procedure, has been applied to behaviour problems such as alcoholism and drug addiction, and is called *aversion therapy*. The aim of this is to get the patient to develop an adverse reaction to alcohol or drugs by using the vomiting reflex; this can be activated by giving the patient an injection of a vomiting-inducing drug. Drugs which bring on vomiting are called *emetics*.

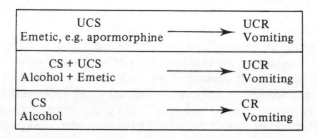

UCS Emetic, e.g. apormorphine	⟶	UCR Vomiting
CS + UCS Alcohol + Emetic	⟶	UCR Vomiting
CS Alcohol	⟶	CR Vomiting

This vomiting is then deliberately associated with drinking alcohol. However, note that it is always a reflex that we condition: the patient cannot stop himself vomiting. He may realize that it is the emetic which is causing the vomiting, but the association between the CS and UCS happens automatically: thinking about it cannot stop it.

Aversion therapy thus assumes that the individual has not sufficiently learnt to avoid alcohol or drugs; the conditioning process enables him to learn this avoidance response. However, as mentioned earlier, other behavioural problems may be caused by an individual's having learnt some kind of 'abnormal' behaviour. Behaviour therapists believe that phobias, for example, are a result of learning and can originate through a process very similar to Classical Conditioning. They argue that lesser fears and other emotions may develop in a similar way. A terrifying experience obviously causes fear and anxiety; according to Classical Conditioning anything which becomes associated with that terrifying experience may thus become a CS and may itself induce fear and anxiety. The table on page 75 shows how a behaviour therapist might interpret the way in which a person's cat phobia could develop.

Such a phobia can last for years and yet in Pavlov's experiment when the CS was presented several times without the UCS the CR was extinguished. Why does this not happen with a phobia? The answer

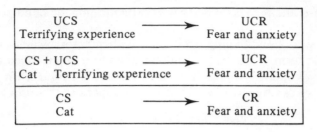

seems to be that the phobic individual never allows himself to get anywhere near the CS – a cat in this case – and will even go to the extreme of refusing to go out of doors, watch television or read a newspaper, in case he sees or hears mention of a cat. In this case of course the CS is not being presented over and over again, either with or without the UCS, so the CR is not extinguished. A behaviour therapist would therefore set up a situation in which extinction can occur and he could do this in two ways:

1 *Flooding* or *implosion therapy*. The patient is locked in a room with the cat; although he will be frightened, eventually the CS–CR bond will extinguish. This can of course be a fairly dangerous procedure, especially when the phobia is very strong, so in general the second method is preferred.

2 *Systematic desensitization*. Instead of being directly exposed to the feared object the patient is only gradually exposed to it: he may be allowed to see it from a distance and gradually move closer, or he may see a series of objects ranging from one which only vaguely resembles the feared object to one which resembles it very closely. In addition, as each object is shown, the patient is trained in various relaxation methods so that he can learn to associate relaxation with each of them in turn. Every time a new object is presented some anxiety will be induced through generalization – the recognition of its similarities to the feared object. But because the patient is now also conditioned to be relaxed whenever he is shown one of these objects, the two responses will cancel each other out. New objects increasingly like the original are introduced and the procedure repeated until eventually the patient's phobia is conquered.

Notice that with this system it is not really necessary to know what the original terrifying experience was; all the behaviour therapist must find out is the type of stimulus that triggers off the fear response, and then he can set about extinguishing the bond between them.

Classical Conditioning deals only with reflexes, which are the simplest form of behaviour, and can therefore be classified as the simplest kind of learning. If we try to design a neural 'wiring diagram' we can hypothesize about what happens in this process.

Figure 30a   Before Conditioning

Possible Changes in Neural Connections

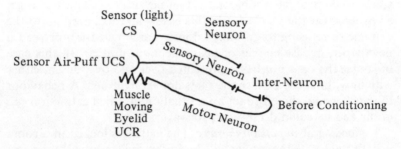

Figure 30b. After Conditioning

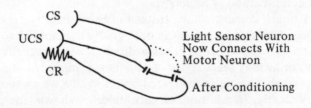

It may be that Classical Conditioning involves the actual joining of the neuron representing the CS to the neuron representing the UCS. Alternatively, the CS neuron may form a bond with the motor neuron that causes the response, directly. If this is what happens the process is another example of the formation of a simple cell assembly.

Classical Conditioning is a very simple form of learning; it may not seem very clever learning to us, but its importance is that it acts as a model of learning. It was, for example, about the earliest description and explanation of how learning can take place, through the association of stimuli and responses.

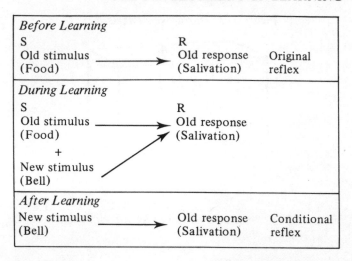

The association of a new stimulus with either the original stimulus or the original response involves a change in behaviour such as the salivation of an animal to the sound of a bell, something that it did not do previously.

But of course Classical Conditioning cannot explain the whole process of learning. When early psychologists tried to use it to explain all learning and behaviour they utterly confused themselves. In order to explain even fairly simple behaviour, such as getting up and opening the door when the door-bell rings, they had to invent such strange terms as 'door-opening reflexes' in order to follow the Classical Conditioning formula. It thus became clear fairly quickly that the model of Classical Conditioning was too inflexible; humans obviously do not require the presentation of stimuli together tens or even hundreds of times before they can associate them. A quicker and more flexible model of learning is therefore required.

Operant Conditioning

The basis of *Operant Conditioning* was discovered by E.L. Thorndike in 1911, shortly after Pavlov's work on Classical Conditioning. Thorndike was studying problem solving in animals, and had devised a 'puzzle box' in which cats had to solve the problem of how to escape (see figure 31a). The solution, of course, is for the cat to pull the loop of string either with its paw or its mouth. This releases the catch, and the spring pulls the door open. Thorndike would put a

Figure 31a. Thorndike's Puzzle Box

Figure 31b. Simplified Graph of Results of Puzzle-box Experiment

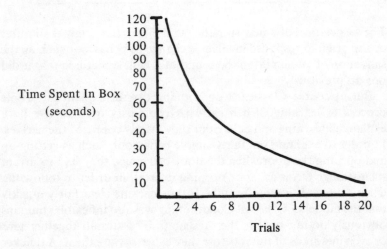

cat into the box and time how long it took the animal to escape. When it had escaped it was put in again, and once more the time it took to escape was noted. When these times were plotted on a graph Thorndike noted that in general, as one might expect, the animal spent less time in the box with each trial. After about twenty trials the cat was able to escape as soon as it was placed in the box. Thorndike put forward the following hypothesis: if a certain response has pleasant consequences, it is more likely than other responses to occur again in the same circumstances. This became known as the *Law of Effect*. Pulling the loop permitted escape, and therefore had 'pleasant consequences' for the cat; it was thus more likely to be repeated than other behaviour which did not lead to escape.

B.F. Skinner is regarded as the father of Operant Conditioning, but his work was based on Thorndike's Law of Effect. Skinner, however, introduced a new term into the Law of Effect – reinforcement, already referred to. Behaviour which is reinforced tends to be repeated: behaviour which is not reinforced tends to die out, or to be extinguished. To reinforce is to strengthen, so behaviour which is strengthened tends to be repeated – obvious enough, perhaps; but Skinner's contribution was to show what sorts of things or events could act as reinforcers. In the first type of experiment described a reinforcer is used in very much the same way as a reward, but it should be remembered that rewards are not the only possible type of reinforcers (see positive and negative reinforcement on page 84).

The term 'Operant Conditioning' was coined by Skinner and roughly means the conditioning of behaviour. An 'operant' is, in effect, an operation which the organism performs on or in its environment – motor behaviour, usually voluntarily performed.

Skinner developed machines for Operant Conditioning which have been named 'Skinner boxes', and in which rats and pigeons are the subjects most often used.

Figure 32. A Skinner Box

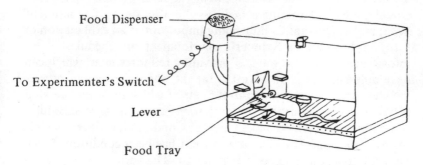

When placed in a Skinner box the animal has to press a lever to open a food tray and thus obtain reinforcement in the form of food. In any situation an animal has a certain repertoire of behaviour; a rat, for example, will show exploratory behaviour when first placed in the Skinner box such as scratching at the walls, sniffing and looking round. By accident in the course of its exploration, it will press the lever and food will be presented. Every time the rat does so it is given food; thus its pressing of the lever is reinforced by the presentation of food, for the animal comes to associate this particular action with receiving this reward. Any other responses such as those mentioned above are not reinforced, and so tend to be extinguished. After several presentations of the reinforcement the rat will press the lever far more often than it did formerly. When the animal has been conditioned in this way we should find that the lever pressing, previously an accidental response, has now become a Conditional Response.

In Classical Conditioning the Unconditional Stimulus itself provides the reinforcement; this is presented before the Conditional Stimulus. In Operant Conditioning, however, the reinforcement is presented after the response. Operant Conditioning, then, uses reinforcement to single out one specific action from the animal's normal behaviour and to ensure that it is repeated more often than the rest. The reinforcement in Classical Conditioning causes the response to be made in the first place. (For other differences between Classical and Operant Conditioning see page 89.)

Schedules of Reinforcement
So far we have described how an animal in the Skinner box which presses the lever receives a pellet of food each time it does so. If we stopped giving this reinforcement the lever-pressing behaviour would gradually be extinguished, usually after only a few minutes. What makes Operant Conditioning important as an explanation of learning, however, is Skinner's development of schedules of reinforcement – different ways of providing reinforcement, which can have different effects on both the rate at which the animal presses the lever, the *response rate*, and the rate at which the lever-pressing behaviour is extinguished, the *extinction rate*. It is these schedules of reinforcement which make Operant Conditioning a very flexible form of learning. Any response, once it has been conditioned, can be made to last as long as it is required. The various schedules of reinforcement and their effects on response rate and extinction rate are described below.

Continuous reinforcement
This is the method used when setting up the conditioning procedure.

Each response is reinforced, but if reinforcement is ceased extinction occurs fairly quickly.

Fixed-ratio reinforcement (FR)
The subject's behaviour is reinforced only after a fixed number of responses. Pigeons in a Skinner box have been known to respond to an FR of 1 : 1,000, or 1 reinforcement per 1,000 responses – commonly written as FR 1,000. This gives a high rate of response and fairly rapid extinction.

Fixed-interval reinforcement (FI)
The subject's behaviour is reinforced only after a fixed period of time, provided at least one response has been made during that period. This method provides a slow rate of response, often only one response per period; for example in an FI 2 schedule, reinforcement is provided every 2 minutes. Often the animal makes a response only in the last few seconds of each 2-minute period. This has a fairly rapid rate of extinction.

Variable-ratio reinforcement (VR)
Reinforcement is given after an average number of responses; for example, a VR 10 schedule is one in which, on average, every 10 responses gain a reinforcement. The actual reinforcement does not arrive on every 10th response, but there will be 3 reinforcements given for 30 responses:

Responses

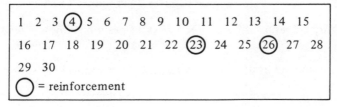

This method provides a steady rate of response which is resistant to extinction: the animal makes many responses before extinction occurs.

Variable-interval reinforcement (VI)
Reinforcement is given, say, every 5 minutes on average, but not

on every 5th minute. A VI 5 reinforcement schedule would look like this, with 3 reinforcements per 15 minutes:

Minutes

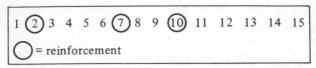

1 ②3 4 5 6 ⑦8 9 ⑩ 11 12 13 14 15
◯ = reinforcement

This provides a steady rate of response, but not as high as with the VR schedule. The response becomes very resistant to extinction: the animal continues to respond for a long time after the reinforcement ceases.

It is obvious that we cannot switch suddenly from a continuous reinforcement schedule to, say, an FR 1,000 schedule; the process has to be a gradual one. For example, to obtain an FR 1,000 schedule the intermediate stages might be FR 5, FR 10, FR 20, FR 50, FR 100, FR 200, FR 300, FR 500 and so on up to FR 1,000.

Effects on Response and Extinction Rates

Schedule	Effect per minute on Response Rate	Effect on Extinction Rate
Continuous	Steady − 5 per min.	Fast
FR Fixed ratio	Fast − FR 5 gives 20 per min.	Fast
FI Fixed interval	Slow − FI 1 gives 2 per min.	Fast
VR Variable ratio	Fast − VR 5 gives 15 per min.	Slow − many responses
VI Variable interval	Steady − VI 5 gives 10 per min	Very slow − long time

Successive Approximation or Behaviour Shaping

All the schedules of reinforcement detailed above are generally used, and are only applicable to a single response. This response, however, can be far more complex than a simple lever-pressing reaction. Skinner, for example, taught – or, more properly, conditioned – pigeons to play ping-pong, and to act as pilots in rockets.

Such feats are achieved by *successive approximation*. Operant Conditioning selects particular actions and by reinforcing them ensures that they are repeated. Once an animal has been conditioned to perform a particular action it tends to use this as the basis of its behaviour and elaborates on it. If, for example, we want a pigeon to turn round and to walk in a left-hand circle, we first reinforce any movement the pigeon makes to the left. It repeats this and elaborates on it, maybe by pecking at the floor, fluttering its wings, and moving its head further to the left. We reinforce only this last response, so that we now have two conditioned acts of behaviour – one the pigeon's turning perhaps 15° to the left, the second a turn of another 20° or so. With two reinforcements we have therefore conditioned the pigeon to turn 35° to the left. If we continue to reinforce only movements that take the pigeon further to the left, eventually the pigeon will turn full circle. The whole process may take as little as five minutes or so. Each successive behavioural action *approximates* – becomes closer – to the final type of behaviour required.

Extinction, Generalization and Discrimination in Operant Conditioning

In Classical Conditioning extinction could be produced by removing the UCS, which was the reinforcer. The same procedure applies in Operant Conditioning but takes time; removing reinforcement completely after, say, a VR 5 schedule will not extinguish the response as quickly as removing the reinforcer after an FR 5 schedule.

Generalization can also occur: a response to stimuli similar to but not identical with the original can be made. The rat in the Skinner box, for example, may have been conditioned to press the left-hand lever but may occasionally generalize the lever-pressing response to the right-hand lever.

Discrimination in a subject can be achieved, and can overcome generalization if desired, using the same principles as those employed in Classical Conditioning. We could, for example, teach the animal to discriminate between a situation in which it will be reinforced for pressing the lever, and one in which it will not; for example, we could condition the animal to press the lever only when the light above the lever is on.

Positive and Negative Reinforcement
You will remember that the formula for Operant Conditioning is:

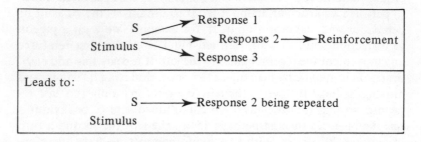

By giving the animal something it wants, such as food, we reinforce response 2. Giving the animal something it wants, needs or likes is called *positive reinforcement*.

The negative-reinforcement formula, however, looks slightly different:

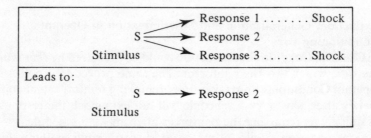

Here, the reinforcement occurs when we stop something which the animal does not like. Thus the presentation of something which the animals wants or needs and the removal of an unpleasant stimulus are both reinforcers, because they both strengthen the required response.

Escape and Avoidance Learning
Learning which is brought about by *negative reinforcement* is termed *escape learning*. For example, an animal is made to stand on an electrified floor grid and is given a mild electric shock; if it jumps or runs away from the grid, the shock stops. Escape behaviour is thus reinforced by the cessation of the painful stimulation. The problem with this type of learning, however, is that it can deal only with

very simple types of behaviour: because the shock produces large emotional responses in the animal it is unlikely to try to do anything more complex or unusual than escape.

However, if we give the animal in the Skinner box a warning buzzer a few seconds before the shock starts we can develop more sophisticated behaviour in the subject. If the animal accidentally moves closer to the lever between the sound of the buzzer and the occurrence of the shock, we stop the shock. The action of approaching the lever is then reinforced by the non-appearance of the shock – it is negatively reinforced – and we can thus shape lever-pressing behaviour. Once this behaviour has been established, it is very resistant to extinction – more so even than VI schedules. This form of learning is called *avoidance learning*. The animal makes a particular response in order to avoid the shock; the particular response is negatively reinforced.

Secondary Reinforcement
In the examples of Operant Conditioning discussed above, food is involved as a reinforcer; it is the main or *primary reinforcer*. However, if we pair another stimulus with the primary reinforcer the second stimulus also acquires reinforcing properties. For example in the Skinner box, when the animal makes a correct response a food tray may click into position with an audible sound. This clicking noise can thus become associated with food because every time the animal hears the click, food appears. In time the animal will perform the required responses while accepting the clicking noise alone as a reinforcer: the sound becomes a *secondary reinforcer*. Something which has been associated with a primary reinforcer – for example food – can thus become a reinforcer too.

You will remember this idea of pairing or associating from the earlier description of Classical Conditioning; the above case is also an example of this. Consider how much more flexible secondary reinforcers can make Operant Conditioning: the reinforcer need not always be a primary one so the range of possible reinforcers can be greatly extended; more or less anything that has been paired with a primary reinforcer can become a secondary reinforcer. Perhaps the most obvious case with humans is that of money which in the past was associated mainly with primary reinforcers: you can use money to buy food and drink. Thus it is now possible to reinforce and induce repetition of behaviour with money. You will notice in chapter 14, however, that although money can be a motivator or reinforcer for people at work it is by no means the only possible one. Social reinforcement such as attention and praise from other people is also a very powerful reinforcer (see also chapter 9). Yet social reinforcers may be an entirely separate kind of reinforcement and perhaps innate; Harlow's experiment concerning love in infant monkeys (see page 131, chapter 8) suggests that this might in fact be the case.

The Use of Operant Conditioning
Operant Conditioning, like Classical Conditioning, is used in the treatment of behaviour disorders. One fairly recent innovation is the use of Operant Conditioning to develop speech in schizophrenics and autistic patients. Nobody really knows yet what the cause of autism is, but it is characterized by a withdrawal from the environment, and seems to affect the individual in childhood. An autistic child does not respond when somebody talks to him, rarely makes an effort to interact with anybody else and could be said to live in a world of his own. Operant Conditioning is now being used to induce autistic children to begin to speak. The basic principle of reinforcing the required behaviour is used to shape into speech patterns what few verbal responses the child does make. Often food is used as a reinforcer, or the opportunity to perform some activity which the child obviously likes. It is difficult to use cuddles or praise with autistic children because they do not often respond to such attention and do not seem even to hear when they are addressed. From time to time even an autistic child makes some kind of noise with his vocal organs, usually grunts, groans or squeals. By using successive approximation, behaviour shaping, the therapist first reinforces those sounds which come closest to words and then uses these as a basis to condition the child actually to utter proper words. The next task is to condition the child to link the words together into sentence form in the hope that once the child begins to do so he will also begin to interact more with his environment and cease to be isolated.

Apparently it is not too difficult to condition an autistic child to utter some words. It is usually possible to persuade him to say one or two in an intensive two-hour session of conditioning; but the therapist often finds difficulty in getting him to string words together into sentence form. Some therapists are now training such children's parents in the techniques of Operant Conditioning so that they can spend several hours a day with the child themselves; such intensive sessions of conditioning might eventually begin to show more useful results.

Biofeedback

Until the mid-1960s it was assumed that Classical and Operant Conditioning were absolutely separate types of learning, the major difference between them being that Classical Conditioning could work only with reflexes and Operant Conditioning could work only with voluntary – non-reflex – behaviour. However, some intriguing experiments in 1969 by N.E. Miller and L.V. DiCara at Rockefeller University in the USA suggested that the differences between Classical and Operant Conditioning are much less great than had been thought. Miller and DiCara used Operant Conditioning to control the activity of parts of the autonomic nervous system in rats. By using behaviour-shaping techniques they were able to alter such involuntary responses as heart-rate, blood-pressure and intestinal contraction – responses it had been assumed it was not possible to control with anything other than Classical Conditioning and then only with difficulty. Miller and DiCara administered a curare-derived drug which paralysed all the voluntary muscles in their subject in order to ensure that any changes in the autonomic responses were not caused by the conditioning of motor responses such as the animal's relaxing or contracting its muscles (experienced practitioners of yoga can alter their heart-rate and blood-pressure, for example, with conscious muscular control). Because the rat was paralysed, food and water could not be used as reinforcers, so, following work by J. Olds, electrodes were implanted in that part of the rat's hypothalamus known as the 'pleasure centre'. Artificial stimulation of this part of the brain is apparently pleasurable, and can be used as a reinforcer. By making a correct response – lowering its heart-rate for example – the animal would be given a brief, mild electrical stimulation to the pleasure centre and this stimulation acted as the reinforcement.

Biofeedback techniques have now become very popular with the general public and the medical profession and machines are commercially available which when used to study humans display EEG traces or galvanic skin-response changes (see pages 9 and 11). An individual can condition himself, for example, to lower his arousal level, by using the knowledge that he is succeeding in doing so as a reinforcement. Research on biofeedback continues at an intense rate.

There are indications that small groups of as few as three or four neurons can be controlled by an individual using biofeedback techniques, and some doctors are now becoming interested in using biofeedback on their patients as a method of controlling high blood-pressure, for example, without the use of drugs.

Programmed Learning

The shaping of human behaviour is similar to, but more complex than, the shaping of animal behaviour because human beings can of course understand quite complicated instructions, and their initial repertoire of behaviour – from which certain responses will be selected – may already be much nearer the required goal. In addition, the range of reinforcers for humans is much wider. In a learning situation, for example, the knowledge that a correct response has been made and therefore that the problem has been understood is reinforcement in itself: a sense of satisfaction is derived from achievement. Acknowledgement of the correctness of a response may be given by a teacher or parent; alternatively a student or child may assess his own performance.

Learning, as we have said, involves a change in behaviour. What makes learning 'better' or more useful is the range of behaviour that can be produced by the new knowledge – the wider the range of behaviour, the better the learning. Operant Conditioning in the form known as *programmed learning* seeks to affect behaviour directly. Pieces of information are given and the student's behaviour is conditioned so that it must show evidence of the understanding of the new information. The correct behavioural responses are reinforced and therefore become more frequent.

In the planning of a learning programme it is essential to predict behaviour; it must be known at which points a student may go wrong. This problem is greatly reduced by breaking down the information into very small steps called *frames*. If the steps are small enough the possible number of responses will be limited, usually to the one correct response. A programme which allows only correct answers is called a *linear programme* – 'linear' referring to the straight sequence of frames. A piece of information is given and immediately tested. As explained, the student's satisfaction at being able to move on is a sufficient reinforcer. We can interpret the basis of programmed learning, using the Operant Conditioning formula (If the studen makes an incorrect answer he is not reinforced and has to repeat the frame that he got wrong.):

The Differences between Classical and Operant Conditioning
In some ways Classical and Operant Conditioning are quite distinct:

Classical Conditioning	Operant Conditioning
Deals only with involuntary behaviour	Deals with voluntary behaviour and involuntary (biofeedback) as well
Reinforcement strengthens the conditional response but is neutral: it works whether or not the organism likes it	Reinforcement strengthens the conditional response and is either positive (something the organism likes) or negative (the removal of an unpleasant stimulus)
The response is elicited by the reinforcer which has to be given before the response is made	Reinforcement is given after the response is voluntarily made, and strengthens it
Little or no weakening of the reinforcement is possible otherwise the response is extinguished. Schedules cannot be used to alter the response and extinction rate	The reinforcer may be greatly diffused, using schedules of reinforcement, to alter the response and extinction rates
A reinforcer can only trigger one type of response, for example, a puff of air across the eye always gives an eye-blink	A reinforcer can be used to strengthen many different responses using shaping techniques
Shows generalization, discrimination, extinction, spontaneous recovery	As Classical Conditioning
Relies on the linking or association of stimuli and responses, S−R	As Classical Conditioning

Trial and Error and the Development of Learning Sets

Remember that one of the criticisms of Classical Conditioning is that it cannot explain all learning; and particularly, that it takes a long time. It must be admitted, however, that under certain conditions – usually when the Unconditional Stimulus is very strong – the conditioning procedure may take place in a single presentation of the CS and UCS. This is sometimes called *single-trial learning*.

Despite the possibilities afforded by one-trial learning, however, Classical Conditioning is not flexible or quick enough to explain all the learning processes which humans can show. Operant Conditioning, including the reinforcement schedules, gives a better explanation; it shows how reinforcement is not necessary on every trial, and also how new forms of behaviour can develop gradually. But to some extent Operant Conditioning is open to the same criticism as Classical Conditioning – that the process of learning takes such a long time.

A list of all the different forms of behaviour which humans can show would be massive. As a hazardous guess adult humans may each have a repertoire of several thousand different kinds of response; yet from this vast repertoire they are able with remarkable speed to select those responses which help them to adapt to or control their environment. Theoretically Operant Conditioning can explain how we develop these large numbers of responses in the first place but it does not seem to be so good at explaining how we are able to select the most efficient and appropriate response from our repertoire.

Thorndike's experiment with the cat's puzzle box (see page 77) showed that learning came gradually as the correct response was reinforced and incorrect or non-reinforced responses were extinguished, but this took time – about twenty trials in the Thorndike experiment. The gradual development of new behaviour by the reinforcement of correct responses and the extinction of incorrect ones is termed *trial-and-error learning*, because with each successive trial the number of errors is reduced until eventually the correct response is the only one left. From your own experience it will seem that you do not have to spend this long working out the answer to a problem, but nothing we have looked at so far gives a really convincing explanation of how we can process so much information so quickly.

Certainly trial and error does play a part in our learning, particularly when we are developing entirely new types of response; but if we really do have several thousand different types of response, trial-and-error learning would surely involve our scanning the whole repertoire of our responses and trying them one by one. This would take a very long time to do. Psychologists studying the development of language in humans, for example, have said that if a child had to learn all the words and different sentence formations in English by trial and error he would reach adult fluency only at the age of a hundred. Because we know children do not take this long, some other process in addition to trial and error must be involved.

At the Primate Laboratory of the University of Wisconsin in 1949 Professor Harry S. Harlow performed some brilliant investigations into how 'short cuts' allied to trial-and-error learning may enable us to apply previous learning to the learning of new things. Both monkeys and children were used as subjects in these experiments. The first type of experiment was a simple discrimination test. Two objects of different size, shape and colour were put in front of the subjects and by the use of straightforward Operant Conditioning they were conditioned to choose one of the objects: a peanut or raisin, or brightly coloured macaroni beads, were placed under the 'correct' object. The subjects learnt to choose the correct object by trial and error and as soon as they were able to choose the correct object immediately, two new objects were substituted and the same process repeated. After many trials involving several hundred different pairs of objects Harlow reported that the subjects learnt each new problem more quickly than the one before until a new problem involving shapes that the subjects had never seen before could be solved in one trial. Harlow found that the children learnt more rapidly than the monkeys but still made the same kinds of error: in fact the fastest monkeys learnt more quickly than the slowest children.

But what was happening here? This was certainly not pure trial-and-error learning, especially not in the later trials. Trial-and-error learning certainly took place in the earlier trials, but after possibly two hundred such trials the subjects were able to pick out the correct objects after only one trial and thereafter continued to pick them, even though they might never have seen the particular pair of objects before.

Consider the behaviour of a monkey after two hundred such trials. It is presented with two shapes it has never seen before, one of which is the 'correct' one; by chance it may pick up the correct object first and if it does so it will pick up the same object every time. If, however, it picks up the incorrect object on the first trial it will immediately pick up the correct object on the next trial and continue to do so from then on. Although pure trial and error was necessary in the earlier problems it is clearly now no longer necessary. The animal seems to have performed quite a sophisticated piece of learning: as a result of having experienced the trial-and-error learning of the earlier tests the monkey seems by this time to have developed some kind of ability to understand the type of problem, or to have understood the principles involved in solving this type of problem.

A further kind of puzzle which Harlow used in his experiment may make this clearer. This time the monkey was presented with three shapes, of which two were the same and one was the 'odd man out'. The monkey's task was to choose the odd man out and once it had learnt to do so three new different shapes were substituted for the old ones. Again after maybe two hundred trials the monkey was able to select the odd man out without any hesitation at all, even when the three shapes in front of it were shapes it had never seen before. The monkey had not learnt simply to pick the odd man out; apparently it had learnt the principle of 'odd man out'. In other words it had learnt not just how to solve a particular problem but how to solve a particular type of problem.

This was Harlow's belief. The rule or rules which enable the subject to solve problems similar in principle to those already solved but which do not use the same objects or elements is called a *Learning Set*. A Learning Set is therefore a way of solving a particular type of problem, and this is why Harlow's experiments and the concept of Learning Sets are important: they provide an explanation of how, by trial and error, we can develop structures which enable us to learn quickly and efficiently.

An experiment in 1941 by Hendrikson and Schroeder also bears out the point that developing a Learning Set is learning the principles by which a type of problem can be solved. Their subjects were boys and they were divided into two groups. The task facing both was to shoot pellets with an air rifle at a target which was submerged in water, but before their target practice one group was given an explanation of the way in which water bends the light by refraction so that the target is not actually in the position in which it appears. The other group received no explanation about refraction. Both

groups were then allowed to shoot at the target and their perform-
ances were compared. There was very little difference in the number
of trials which both groups needed to learn to hit the target, but
once both groups were able to hit it the depth of water covering the
target was increased, which in turn increased the refraction. Under
these circumstances the group who had had refraction explained to
them performed much better than the other group, learning to hit
the deeper target in fewer attempts.

Operant Conditioning proved to be more useful in the explanation
of human learning than did Classical, and the work on Learning
Sets suggests the possibility that some fairly complex rules may be
learnt by trial and error. However, the ability of an individual to
learn depends on more than the presence or absence of reinforcement. Account needs to be taken of the individual's capacity to learn
and it is the development of this which is discussed in the following
chapter.

Summary

1 Learning is a relatively permanent change in behaviour as a result
of experience.
2 Classical Conditioning (Pavlov) is probably the simplest form of
learning, and is based on reflexes. The organism can be conditioned
to make a Reflex Response to a different stimulus by repeated
presentation of this new (Conditional) Stimulus with the original
(Unconditional) Stimulus. If the Conditional Stimulus is continually
presented alone the Conditional Response will gradually become
weaker and stop; this is known as extinction. The organism will
generalize the response to stimuli similar to the Conditional
Stimulus, but generalization can be overcome by discrimination
conditioning.
3 Classical Conditioning may provide an explanation of how fears
and anxieties can develop, and has been used by behaviour therapists
to remove phobias, or to develop aversions to undesirable
behaviour.
4 Operant Conditioning (Skinner) is based on Thorndike's Law of
Effect, and shows that responses which are reinforced by something
an animal wants, needs or likes are repeated. Negative reinforcement
involves the removal of unpleasant stimulation when the correct
response has been made. It can deal with voluntary behaviour and

with involuntary behaviour, using biofeedback techniques. Schedules of reinforcement and successive approximation or behaviour shaping make it a very flexible technique.

5 Operant Conditioning can be used, for example, in the shaping of speech in autistics; it is the basis of programmed learning.

6 Harlow's work on trial-and-error learning and Learning Sets suggests how Operant Conditioning can enable an individual to learn not only single facts or responses but rules and principles.

Chapter 6

The Development of the Intellect

Jean Piaget's Theories

We have seen that Harlow's work describes how from very simple beginnings and simple trial-and-error learning an animal or a person can develop the ability to do not just a particular task but a particular type of task. Thus children in school learn addition sums but do not have to learn every possible one that they will ever come across; they learn, as a result of trial and error, the principle of addition. Using Hebb's theory, discussed in chapter 4, imagine a phase sequence gradually developing that enables a child to do addition sums. The more practice the child has in doing them the stronger this phase sequence will become and the more easily it can be applied to a particular type of problem, that of adding numbers together.

Jean Piaget, a Swiss psychologist, whose work has been largely concerned with how children's intellects develop, proposes that the development of the child is not necessarily a continuous process. He has tried to identify fairly well-defined stages of development through which the child passes, stages in which his behaviour can be seen to be different from that in earlier stages. He stresses that all children will go through the various stages in the same sequence but not necessarily at the same ages; the following age groups must therefore be viewed as approximations of the ages at which the various stages begin and end.

The Sensorimotor Stage

The first, or *sensorimotor*, stage, runs roughly from birth to two years old. The child is at first unable to predict the environment: if an object goes out of view, it no longer exists for him. Behaviour consists mainly of reflexes but gradually develops into voluntarily controlled movements such as directed groping with the hands or brushing unwanted objects aside.

The Pre-Operational Stage

The *pre-operational* phase generally runs from two to seven years. With the development of language and memory the child is able to remember more about the environment and is beginning to be able to predict it better. These predictions are still simple ones and the child tends to over-generalize, calling all men 'daddy', for example. He is still tied to the appearance of things and has not yet learnt flexibility in the application of rules about how the environment works. For example, a litre of water in a tall, thin glass compared with a litre of water in a short, large-diameter glass would appear to a child to be more in volume. This is because he cannot *conserve* volume: in other words he has not yet learnt the rule that the shape of an object can change, though its volume does not.

The Concrete Operational Stage

In the *concrete operational* period from seven to eleven years, the child is still dependent on the appearance of objects but is becoming able to learn more sophisticated rules about the environment. He has now learnt the rules of conservation and can use simple logic to solve problems, provided that they involve real objects. He can, for example, put a number of different-sized dolls into order of size but cannot solve the same type of problem when it is presented verbally; for example Gladys is taller than Freda, Freda is taller than Mary. Who is the shortest?

The Formal Operational Stage

The *formal operational* phase covers the period from eleven years to adulthood. The child learns the more sophisticated rules in this time. He can now develop general laws and scientific reasoning. His thoughts are no longer always tied to the concrete; he can form hypotheses and make rules about abstract things. The learning of new rules does not end with the ending of childhood, but continues throughout life.

Thus the child's intellectual ability gradually develops as it progresses through the various stages until it reaches the formal operational stage. This is fine as far as it goes; it is a description of what happens. But how is the child able to progress through the various stages? What happens inside his brain? How is he able to learn these new forms of behaviour? Piaget says that the child's intellectual development takes place through the development of what he calls *schemata*. These are hypothetical constructions; Piaget says little about what form they take inside the brain but if you compare the formation of a schema with the formation of a cell assembly, phase sequence or Learning Set it will give you an appreciation of how the system works. Piaget believes that the reason for the development of the child's intellect and learning ability is his need to cope with his environment, and enlargement and formation of schemata are the basis for his increasing ability to predict and control it. There seem to be two main ways in which schemata develop – *assimilation* and *accommodation*.

Assimilation

This refers to the way in which an existing schema can be used to solve problems or perform tasks which are new but similar in type to those which have been dealt with in the past. Suppose that you have already developed a schema for bicycle riding. This schema contains the necessary elements and skills – the ability to balance, steer, turn the pedals and work the brakes, as well as road sense and so on. Suppose you now wish to ride a motorbike. Many of the skills involved in your bicycle-riding schema can be used, with little or no alteration, in riding a motorbike. To a certain extent you will already be equipped to ride a motor-cycle; an already-existing schema can be used to perform new kinds of behaviour. In effect you 'assimilate' – take in – information that the new task is broadly similar to a skill which you already possess (see figure 33). Harlow's experiment with monkeys' development of Learning Sets (see page 9) illustrated the same process – the adaptation of an existing ability or schema to a new odd-man-out problem.

Accommodation

You will probably have realized that the description of the bicycle and motorbike-riding schema is rather one-sided. In real life, although the bicycle-riding schema would probably help you considerably in learning to ride a motorbike, it would not remove the need to learn something about the new skill; for example, it would not help you much with clutch control or gear-changing, or the operation of the engine itself. In order to be able to cope properly with riding a motorbike, you would have to learn this information (see figure 33). This is what is meant by 'accommodation'; schemata have to be altered, or sometimes whole new schemata have to be developed, to accommodate new information and skills.

If an existing schema can, by itself, cope with a new situation, the fact that this is possible can simply be built into the schema. Thus in the Learning Sets example on page 92, when the monkey is able to pick the odd man out from three shapes it has never seen before, the information that the problem and the solution with these three shapes has followed the same rule is built into the odd-man-out schema.

Figure 33. Push-bike and Motorbike Schemata

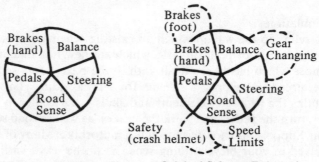

'Push-Bike-Riding' Schema   Original Schema Enlarged
                                   By Accommodation To
                                   Become 'Motorbike-
                                   Riding' Schema

Piaget believes that at birth a child's behaviour consists largely of reflexes, but that it also has a tendency to organize its reflexes and actions – a tendency to adapt to its environment. One of the earliest schemata which Piaget noted was in his own son Laurent, whose basic grasping reflex developed into a sequence of actions involving clasping and unclasping of the hands. Such schemata are easily recognizable forms of behaviour which often occur as recognized wholes and are frequently repeated. Because they are repeated often they can occur when the child is faced with a new situation. One often sees that when young babies have developed the ability to reach for, grasp, and bring an object to their mouths, they often do this with any new object or material. On some occasions, for example when the object brought to the mouth is food, the schema proves useful; then the information that this whole class of objects – any food – can be dealt with satisfactorily by the schema is assimilated into the schema itself. In this way schemata help even very young children to cope better with their environment.

, Thus Piaget's proposed stages of intellectual development result from the development of existing schemata, or assimilation, and of new schemata, or accommodation, which helps the child to predict, control and adapt to its environment successfully. Referring back to the descriptions of the Piagetian developmental stages on page 95, it is now evident that they are in fact lists of the main types of schemata which Piaget supposes develop at the various stages.

Piaget stresses the importance of these stages. Different children go through the same stages in the same order; a child could not first develop the concrete operational schemata and then develop the pre-operational schemata. In this sense, Piaget's theory is maturational and biologically based: the development of the intellect depends on the development of the child's nervous system. If it is true that the development of a child's intellect is a biologically-based maturational process, we should expect the type of environment and experience which a child has to have little effect on the rate at which he goes through the various stages or on the order of the stages themselves. As the Dennis and Dennis study of Hopi Indian children showed (see page 127) a child will be able to walk when the body systems responsible for walking are mature; it is not much use trying to teach it to walk before maturation is complete. Piaget takes a similar view of intellectual development: it is not possible to accelerate the rate of a child's intellectual development to any large extent. Variations in the ages at which different children go through the different stages are probably caused by the types of environment in which they live, and by their cultural and educational experiences. The development of an individual's intellectual abilities, then, is affected by the interaction between the individual and his or her environment; but according to Piaget the maturational basis of this development allows the child to assimilate and accommodate the information and actions afforded by the environment only when it is mature enough to do so (see the parallels with the work of Konrad Lorenz and Tinbergen on Critical Periods in development, chapter 8).

Jerome Bruner's Theories

Bruner's attitude towards intellectual development broadly resembles that of Piaget, but there are also some important and fairly fundamental differences. Piaget's work is largely concerned with the description of what happens; he discusses the mechanisms by which intellect develops mainly in order to clarify the descriptions themselves. Bruner, on the other hand, concerns himself much more with questions about how and why intellectual development occurs. While Piaget regards maturational processes as being probably the most important factors, and culture and education as modifying factors, Bruner places much more emphasis on these last two. He disagrees with Piaget's view that the major motivator or influence in intellectual growth is biological and argues that, if biological development 'pushes' the individual towards more adaptable behaviour, the environment 'pulls' him in the same direction. Here Bruner is stressing that simply to study the child without also examining his experience and environment is bound to give an incomplete picture. Where Piaget simply states that intellectual development involves an interaction between individual and environment, Bruner stresses the point, and regards the child's environment as being rather like a loudspeaker, amplifying the child's abilities.

However, like Piaget, Bruner believes that the developing child plays an active part in its own development; although the family, the educational system and the child's friends, for example, obviously have an influence on development, the child makes his own sense of the world. Remember from chapter 4 that perception is an active, constructive process; from the raw sensory information, we make inferences and draw conclusions about what is really 'out there'. Just as we process stimuli and put our own interpretations on them, so, Bruner argues, do we develop our cognitive abilities in order to understand and interact more successfully with our environment.

To be able to control our environment we have to learn to predict it and in order to be able to do that, we have to be able to pick out reliable patterns, of which the earliest are the constancies, in the events which affect us. So we have to learn to represent and internally organize our experiences. Bruner has been very interested in how we develop the ability to represent our environment internally and use this information to predict what will happen next. He has identified three types of representation which he believes are the basis of cognitive development. They will be described in the order in which they appear in humans; they should be compared with Piaget's developmental stages: Piaget's proposed stages describe what the child himself is biologically capable of doing, whereas Bruner's types of representation are more concerned with the changes in the individual's interpretation or prediction of his environment.

Enactive Representation

The first type of representation to appear in the child is termed by Bruner *enactive representation*. A useful way to think of this type is to regard it as 'motor' or 'muscle memory'. Past experiences cannot yet be stored in symbolic form: a baby can represent past experiences only in the form of motor patterns. It might, for example, at one time have had a string of rattling beads strung across its cot, and could make them rattle by hitting them with its hands. You might notice that when they are taken away it continues to move its hands as if to hit them. It seems to show that it has some form of internal representation of its experience with the beads, and indicates this in motor form, by repeating the motor patterns associated with them. No images of the beads need to be involved; this earliest form of internal representation does not seem to require the use of visual images. Similarly most people say that they can often drive a car 'unconsciously', by which they mean that they do not have to pay attention to every motor movement they make. They have, in effect, a 'muscle memory' which they can use to guide their limb movements. An old party game requires people to describe a helter-skelter without using their hands, and most people find it very difficult to do so. Even adults store helter-skelter information using enactive representation. So it must be with babies' earliest representations of their environments.

Iconic Representation

The second type of representation to appear is termed *iconic representation* – 'icon' meaning 'likeness'. The child now develops the ability to retain images – visual, auditory or tactile – as a faithful representation of the stimuli that reach its sense organs. This method is a very good way of storing information about the environment, but it can have its drawbacks. In the following hypothetical experiment, suppose we use a group of children who relied mainly on iconic

Figure 34. Type of Figure Used by Kuhlman (1)

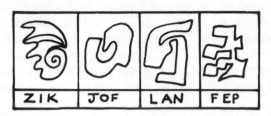

representation, and another group who did not; the former group would be expected to do better at learning to attach the artificial names to the pictures in figure 34.

In 1960 Kuhlman indeed found this result. Children who use iconic imaging are able to make a fairly faithful representation of the picture plus the label, and to recall it when required. Non-imaging children, on the other hand, and those who are not very good at imaging, seem to find it difficult to remember the label and to fit it to the correct picture because the words themselves do not indicate at all which picture they fit. This ability to make faithful representations – although it may seem to be a heavensent gift if you have to learn psychology notes for an examination – can in fact create problems for children who possess it. These arise because iconic imaging is too inflexible: it usually allows a child to learn only specific images of parts of the environment and makes it difficult for him to extract from them the underlying similarities between objects. Thus children who use iconic imaging seem to find it more difficult than non-imagers to categorize things. Kuhlman showed this in another part of the experiment already described. The imagers and non-imagers were each given a series of pictures and all were asked to determine what each of the pictures had in common (see figure 35). The answer is, of course that they are all dwelling-places.

Figure 35. Type of Figure Used by Kuhlman (II)

Non-imaging children had little difficulty in picking out this common factor, but imaging children, just because they were so tied to the pictorial images, found it harder to think beyond the pictures and to extract the significance from them.

Symbolic Representation

The problem with both enactive and iconic representation is that they are relatively inflexible: enactive representation enables the child to interpret the environment only in the form of motor patterns, while iconic representation enables him to represent his environment only in the form of photograph-like images. Because the environment is constantly changing these two forms, with their usefulness only for individual movements or fixed images, cannot effectively code enough information about the environment to enable predictions to be made.

Symbolic representation, however, overcomes this problem by using symbols, as the name suggests. A symbol is something which represents something else; for example, the handshake we exchange with somebody we meet originally symbolized the idea that we would not attack him (we usually shake hands with the right hand, which would normally hold a weapon in a situation of hostility). Bruner thus believes that human language provides a series of symbols in the form of words and sentences with which we can represent and store information about the ever-changing environment: the word 'vegetable' may be just a series of letters printed on a piece of paper, but if you can read and interpret their meaning they contain, and remind you of, a large amount of information – lists of different vegetables and their description; memories of how they taste; how to grow and cook them, and so on. The single word 'vegetable' therefore enables you to store a large amount of information about your environment. Words in themselves are only squiggly marks on paper, or breath expelled from the mouth, but they symbolize information very effectively.

When we develop language, therefore, we develop a collection of efficient, information-storing symbols. Moreover these symbols, because they are not applicable only to the simple characteristics of single objects, can contain information about whole classes of objects. Thus in symbolic representation two major information-storage systems seem to be used – *categorization* and the formation of *hierarchies*.

Categorization

The vegetable example is a case of categorization: 'vegetable' refers not to a specific potato which we once ate, but to a whole realm of edible objects. As another example, consider the category 'cat'. All the figures in figure 36 are recognizable as members of the cat category, yet they are all different: one has no tail; one has a leg

Figure 36. All Different, But All Cats

missing; they have different types of coat, colour, and so on. If you were shown each picture in turn and asked to say what it was, you would have no difficulty in deciding that it was a cat even though the pictures you saw were of markedly different sizes, shades and postures. Your possession of the ability to categorize, however, has enabled you to look beyond the differences in the sensory information and pick out the common factors belonging to the category.

The Formation of Hierarchies

In addition, however, symbolization enables us to construct hierarchies in order to store information, a process which can be illustrated by the results of an experiment conducted by Bower in 1969. The individuals in a group of subjects were given a list of 112 words to learn, and for them the words were arranged into a hierarchy; they were all connected with places to live and the hierarchy imposed some logical order on them, for example 'room', 'flat', 'house', 'street', 'hamlet', 'village', 'town', 'city', 'metropolis', 'county', 'country', 'continent', and so on. A second group learnt the same 112 words, but for this group they were not hierarchically structured. Both groups were allowed to repeat their lists over and over again until they could repeat them correctly. As soon as they had got them right they were not allowed to continue memorizing them. After a time interval both groups were asked to recall as much as they could of the lists. The group with the hierarchically structured list recalled 73 out of the original 112 words while the group without the hierarchies could recall only 21 of the total. The formation of hierarchies and categorization, then, help us to store and retrieve a large amount of information effectively.

An experiment in 1966 by J.S. Bruner and H. Kenney confirms how effective symbolic representation is in helping us to store and use information about our environment (see figure 37 overleaf). The subjects were children whose ages ranged from five to seven years, the younger ones using mainly iconic representation while the older ones could use symbolic representation. The glasses used in the task were graded and placed in order according to both height and diameter; the experimenter first removed a few glasses and then asked the children to replace them, which all managed to do. Similarly when the glasses were mixed up and replaced out of position, all the children could put them back in their original places. Next, however, all the glasses were removed, and only one glass was placed in a different square. The children were then asked to replace the rest of the glasses so as to complete the new pattern (see figure 37). The older children – those capable of symbolic representation – could perform this task satisfactorily but the iconic representers could not. Their iconic representation helped them when asked to remake the original pattern, but because their images were of the original order, they were of little use to them in helping to solve the problem when the new arrangement did not match their images; they were not able to go beyond the bare image of the problem and to deduce that the relationships between the sizes of the glasses were important, and consequently they could not solve the problem when looking at it from a different viewpoint.

Figure 37. Bruner and Kenney's Experiment

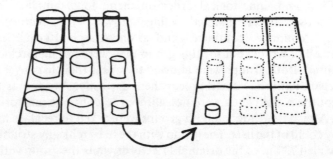

Bruner regards language as an important aid in developing symbolic representation because language enables us to form categories and hierarchies. Although much of Bruner's work parallels that of Piaget, it is partly on the importance of language that their views differ. Piaget originally regarded language as relatively unimportant in the formation of intellectual abilities; however, he has more recently moved towards the view that thought and language develop as separate systems but that the existence of language helps the child's intellect to develop faster, and with greater breadth.

Piaget	Bruner
Sensorimotor	Enactive representation
Pre-operational Concrete operational	Iconic representation
Formal operational	Symbolic representation

Summary

1 Piaget proposed that the ability to learn matures in four main stages – sensorimotor, pre-operational, concrete operational and formal operational – through the formation and enlargement of cognitive structures called schemata. As the child develops stage by stage his behaviour becomes more complex, and this enables the individual to adapt to the environment more successfully.

2 Bruner's views parallel those of Piaget but he describes the three major ways in which the individual stores and uses or represents information about the environment – enactive, iconic and symbolic representation. Symbolic representation is the most flexible, but requires the use of language to enable the categorization of information. Consequently Bruner stresses the importance of language much more than does Piaget.

Chapter 7

The Nature/Nurture Debate on Intelligence and IQ

What is Intelligence?

It seems reasonable first to ask the question, what is *intelligence*? The simple answer is that we do not know.

Consider two different people – a university professor and a lorry driver. Can both of them show 'intelligent' behaviour? We would assume that they can: the university professor may talk 'intelligently' and the lorry driver may be an 'intelligent' driver. Have they then the same amount of 'intelligence'? People might feel inclined to say that the professor is more intelligent than the lorry driver. What, then, is there in the professor's behaviour which might lead us to believe that he is more intelligent?

This is where the problems of definition begin. Most people have an idea of what they mean by intelligence – 'cleverness', 'understanding', 'the ability to think', 'the ability to cope', 'inborn brilliance', and so on. But such definitions do not really enable us to judge whether certain behaviour is either intelligent or unintelligent. The difficulties arise because we are wrongly assuming that intelligence is a thing: accepted descriptions of people – 'He went to university because he's intelligent' or 'She's intelligent: she's got a high IQ' – assume that we each possess a quantity of something called 'intelligence'. But psychologists study behaviour, and most of them therefore really use the term 'intelligence' in the sense of intelligent behaviour. It is impossible to have an amount of intelligence. In grammatical terms perhaps we should think only of 'intelligent' as the adjective, describing behaviour, rather than the noun 'intelligence', which would denote an object.

All the psychologists' attempts to define what is meant by intelligent behaviour have had their critics. Here is a brief summary of three major definitions. C. Spearman believed that intelligence was a thing, and called it a 'general capacity for thinking and reasoning'. L.L. Thurstone, on the other hand, saw intelligence as a series of separate abilities rather than a thing. He believed that abilities such as numerical ability, memory and word fluency together made up intelligent behaviour. Some psychologists have gone further than Thurstone. J.P. Guildford, for example, claimed that intelligence is made up of 120 different factors. The argument about the number of abilities involved in intelligence still continues.

An Operational Definition
Because it is so difficult to find a generally agreed definition of intelligent behaviour, some psychologists have tackled the problem another way. They have devised tests which sample aspects of behaviour; these involve reasoning-type problems, the successful solution of which can then be termed intelligent behaviour. So that which is tested is given the operational definition of intelligence. Note, however, that such tests do not attempt to measure the whole of an individual's behaviour, a well-nigh impossible task; they sample behaviour. If problems are graded in difficulty a test can furthermore be used to compare the problem-solving abilities of different individuals. Suppose that we gave a test of this kind to three subjects, X, Y and Z, and that they scored 90, 90 and 100 respectively out of 120. If X was 8, Y was 10, and Z was 12 years old, comparison of their scores would not of course tell us much about how relatively intelligent their behaviour was as sampled in the test. But if we gave the test to people of the same age group or to large numbers of people of different ages we could find out the levels of difficulty of problems certain age groups could successfully solve.

If in a particular test we find that the 8-year-olds can get an average of 80 answers correct out of 100, the 10-year-olds 90, and the 12-year-olds 120, we can then compare the original subjects X, Y and Z with children of their own ages:

X (aged 8) scored 90	Average for 8-year-olds 80
Y (aged 10) scored 90	Average for 10-year-olds 90
Z (aged 12) scored 100	Average for 12-year-olds 120

We can see that X has performed better than the average for his age, Y has performed the same as the average for his age, and Z has performed worse than the average for his age. We can draw further conclusions from these scores; for example, if we say that

children of physical or chronological age (CA) 8 who score 80 therefore also have a mental age of 8, then X, who scored more than the
average for his age group, must have a mental age above 8; in fact
he has reached the score made by most 9-year-olds, and can therefore
be said to have a mental age of 9.

If we divide mental age by chronological age – and multiply the
result by 100 to eliminate decimal points – we get the following
results:

$$X \quad \frac{9}{8} = 1.125, \text{ i.e. } 113$$

$$Y \quad \frac{9}{10} = 0.9, \text{ i.e. } 90$$

$$Z \quad \frac{10}{12} = 0.83, \text{ i.e. } 83$$

Thus by comparing an individual's score in the test with the scores
of other people of the same age we can arrive at a figure relative
to 100 which indicates how well that individual has performed relative to his contemporaries. This figure – 113 for X, 90 for Y and
83 for Z – is called the *intelligence quotient* or IQ.

But is this a measurement of intelligence? It cannot be, because
it does not measure the whole of intelligence; it measures only a
sample of what is termed, by common consent among psychologists,
intelligent behaviour. Thus somebody with an IQ of 150 is not twice
as intelligent as somebody with an IQ of 75 because it is not the whole
of their intelligence that has been measured; in addition the IQ score
is not an absolutely accurate 'mental ruler': it has a margin of error,
usually of 2 to 3 points. Thus an IQ score of 110 really indicates that
the individual's IQ is somewhere between 107 and 113.

IQ tests were first widely used by A. Binet in the early 1900s as
an instrument for the Education Department of Paris. Their major
purpose was to single out those children who were unlikely to benefit
from the school system of the day; in effect, the Binet test was a
test for mental retardation: children who failed to gain high enough
scores were not allowed to go to school. More modern versions, in
particular the Terman-Merrill version, are still being used today for
selection purposes. The intelligence test in the eleven-plus selection
system is a direct descendant of Binet's test, and is used for much
the same purpose. 'Intelligence test' is, of course, a misleading term,

for the reasons already given. What such tests do sample seems to be mainly the capacity for logical thought, reasoning ability, and speed of thought. Because there is not yet an absolute definition of intelligence nobody can say how important these aspects are in relation to the total range of our intelligent behaviour; but the IQ test can nevertheless be useful in predicting the likelihood of scholastic success, and also in identifying individuals with learning problems.

IQ, we have seen, is only an operational definition of intelligence. In chapter 5 it was stated that in order to include the whole range of phenomena which can be called learning, its definition must be fairly vague. The following similarly vague definition of intelligence was devised by Alice Heim, a psychologist working at Cambridge University who has herself developed several intelligence tests: 'Intelligent activity consists in grasping the essentials in a situation and responding appropriately to them.' This definition – or perhaps more accurately, description – of intelligence, although necessarily vague-sounding, does not make intelligence into a thing; can include most if not all acts of intelligent behaviour; and is still compatible with common conceptions. Thus Heim's description of intelligent behaviour seems the best way of characterizing intelligence available in our present state of knowledge. You will note, too, that it has fairly close parallels with the ideas of Piaget and Bruner on cognitive development – the idea of the individual making efforts to deal effectively with his or her environment.

The Nature/Nurture Debate on Intelligence

This area of research is one which is fraught with difficulties, biases and statistical juggling. In a book of this length we can therefore expect only to try to cover some of the main points in the argument, and to describe some of the methods of investigation used. First, however, several points should be emphasized. Although many of these studies throw light on the nature/nurture debate on intelligence, the vast majority still used IQ as the operational definition of intelligence. Secondly, the nature/nurture debate on intelligence is not really about whether heredity *or* environment is the cause of the development of intelligence; the question is rather one of their relative importance in the development of differences in intelligence. Consider the way in which the area of a rectangle is calculated: the length is multiplied by the breadth. Which of these two measurements is the more important in determining the area of the reactangle? What would happen to the area if either of the two were removed? The rectangle would no longer exist; a line would remain. If the term 'heredity' is substituted for length; 'environment' for breadth; and 'intelligence' for area, their relationship with one another can be seen to be the same. Without either heredity or environment there would be no intelligent behaviour; both are necessary, and a reduction in the influence of either would presumably lead to a reduction in intelligent behaviour.

The hereditary and environmental factors which thus both affect the development of intelligent behaviour actually begin to interrelate from the time of conception and, as we shall see later, it may be possible for environmental factors to have an effect even before conception. To illustrate the impossibility of extreme positions in the nature/nurture debate, imagine the removal of its entire environment from a fertilized egg. Food and oxygen supply would disappear and the egg would then die. Then imagine the removal of the entire hereditary component. That would mean no fertilized egg at all.

We shall now look at investigations in the debate. An attempt was made by D.O. Hebb in 1949 to describe the contributions of the hereditary and environmental components, and the ways in which they affect one another.

Intelligence A, Intelligence B and Intelligence C

Hebb argued that much of the misunderstanding about intelligence arose because two separate facts were not recognized:

1 Humans have brains and brain cells for whose structure and function there must be some genetic blueprint. Presumably also encoded in the genetic blueprint is the ability of these cells to join together to form cell assemblies and phase sequences under certain conditions. In effect, we have an innate ability to form cell assemblies.

2 Although we may have the potential for forming such brain connections we may not necessarily actually do so to the fullest extent: the environment may help or hinder their formation.

In other words, not only must we have brains and potential neural connections within the brain, but we must also actually make these connections. Therefore, according to Hebb, we ought to recognize two distinct types of intelligence.

Intelligence A
This means potential intelligence – the genetically determined structure of the brain and the potential ability of the brain neurons to connect. This potential intelligence is laid down in an individual's genetic blueprint. The fertilized egg has the genetic blueprint or potential for the development of the ten thousand million brain neurons and their ability to connect. What happens to the organism after conception can either help this potential to be realized, or hinder it; it cannot alter the potential itself.

Intelligence B
This describes the extent to which this genetic potential has been realized as a result of the interaction of an individual's genetic make-up with the effects of his environment.

To indicate how complex the interaction between heredity and environment is, consider what happens to the newly fertilized egg. In minute one it is immediately affected by the environment – the conditions of implantation in the womb, and food and oxygen supply, for example. It is now no longer a simple reproduction of genetic information: some of the genetic blueprint has been reproduced, but some has either not been reproduced at all, or has been reproduced imperfectly. The organism at minute two no longer shows only genetic potential: it is the result of the effects of the environment at that time on the structures which are currently developing. It is a different organism from minute one. But at minute two this new organism is still being affected by its environment, to produce yet a different basis at minute three, on which the environment will have further effects. At minute four it will be different again, and so on.

Intelligence B is thus, according to Hebb, the way in which the brain functions after the environment has helped or hindered its development from the genetic blueprints of its cells: it is the average level of performance or comprehension on the part of the developing individual that we infer from his or her behaviour.

We cannot directly study intelligence A: how can you study a potential until it has been realized? We could perhaps devise systems for measuring the neural 'connectability' of an individual's brain, but because we could not do this until neurons had formed, the environment would already have had an effect. Nor is intelligence B measurable. Hebb regards intelligence B as the normal functioning of the brain; thus although it is theoretically possible to monitor separately the activity of each brain neuron, the entire process for an entire brain would take roughly fourteen million years. Even then we should not know what connection each of the neurons had with intelligent behaviour.

Intelligence tests, Hebb says, measure only a sample of intelligence B, so that it is impossible for them to give us reliable information about the nature of intelligence A.

Intelligence C
Philip Vernon, a British psychologist, has proposed a third type, intelligence C. This, he says, is an unknown amount of intelligence B which can be measured with IQ tests. IQ tests cannot measure the whole of an individual's intelligence B, as we have seen, because intelligence B is the way the individual responds to the environment as a whole. Vernon therefore argues that because intelligence C is an unknown proportion of intelligence B, and B is an unknown proportion of A, it is most unwise to use IQ – intelligence C – scores to find out about intelligence A; we do not know anything about the relationship between intelligence C and A (see figure 38).

Figure 38. The Hebb–Vernon Model of Intelligence

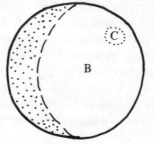

The Entire Area of the Figure Represents Intelligence A

Twin Studies
Towards the end of the last century, Francis Galton performed a series of family studies. He found that intelligent high-IQ parents tended to have offspring with high IQs and that tracing a family over a series of generations showed a remarkable consistency in the type of people in each generation. At first many people might take this as evidence of the importance of heredity in characteristics such as intelligence. A longer consideration makes us question this. Intelligent

parents may pass on 'intelligent' genes to their children but their environment may also differ from the kind provided by less intelligent parents: a child may see more books, have a different kind of conversation with his parents, and so on. However, precisely because of this we cannot use family studies alone for valid evidence in the nature/nurture debate: the child's IQ may be a result of either nature or nurture, or both.

What we can do, however, is to use twins to study how much heredity and environment contribute to differences in IQ.

Figure 39. Twin Study Experimental Design

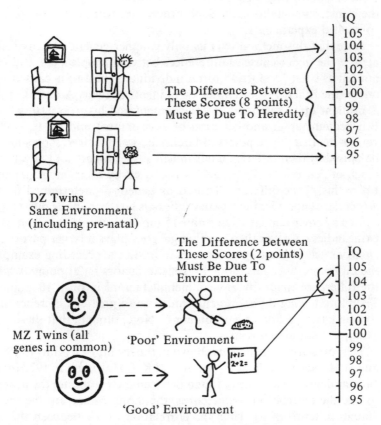

What follows is a rule whose basis can be applied to most of the studies we have mentioned, in order to see if they are accurate and whether or not their findings can be trusted. If we want to distinguish between the effects of heredity and those of environment we can do so in two main ways. If we can obtain two individuals who have had absolutely identical environments, any differences in their intelligence must be caused by hereditary factors. Alternatively, if we can find two individuals with absolutely identical genes and bring them up in different environments, any differences in their intelligence must be caused by environmental factors. In other words, to be able to compare the IQs of two individuals with a view to finding out whether environment or heredity plays the larger part in the differences in their intelligence, we must either control their environment and allow their genes to vary or control their genes and allow their environments to vary. Such procedures form the basis of all controlled experiments.

Note that this method tells us only whether genetics or environment is the major cause of differences between people's IQs. It does not tell us what proportion of an individual's total IQ is caused by one or the other. For example, using identical twins A and B, if A is brought up in one kind of environment and his IQ is 110, while B is brought up in another kind of environment and his IQ is 90, we can say that the 20 points difference between their IQ scores must be caused by their different environments. We still do not know how much of A's 110 or B's 90 points is caused by their environment. From this, if the difference caused by genetics – determined from *dizygotic*, or non-identical, twin studies – is larger than the difference caused by environment – determined from *monozygotic*, or identical, twin studies – we can then say that genetics plays a larger part than environment in creating differences in IQ. In the preceding example the difference brought about by genetic factors is 20 points while the difference made by environmental factors is only 10 points. Therefore having different genes must cause greater differences in IQ than having different environments. Note, though, that these are examples, not actual results.

The correlation coefficients shown in the results of C. Burt in 1953 and H.H. Newman, F.N. Freeman and K.J. Holzinger in 1928 indicate the degree of similarity found between their subjects: the nearer to one the correlation coefficient is, the more similar are the individuals in terms of IQ. Thus the correlation of 0.9 between the IQ of monozygotic twins shows that if one twin has a high IQ then the other is very likely also to have a high IQ. You will notice that the IQs of dizygotic twins and siblings, or brothers and sisters, have lower correlations: the lower the correlation, the less similar are the IQs of the individuals in each pair.

Study of	Correlation Coefficient	
	Burt	Newman, Freeman and Holzinger
Monozygotic twins reared together	0.92	0.91
Monozygotic twins reared apart	0.84	0.67
Dizygotic twins reared together	0.53	0.64
Siblings reared together	0.49	No figures available

These results thus suggest that the IQs of monozygotic twins are more similar than those of dizygotic twins, even when dizygotic twins have lived in the same environments and monozygotic twins in different environments. Heredity must therefore be more important than environment in causing differences in IQ between individuals.

However, it is so difficult to ensure identical environments for DZ twins that some researchers assume part of the IQ differences between such twins are caused by environmental factors. The 'subtraction sum' below can lessen this possibility.

IQ difference between DZ twins (Due to heredity and environment)	−	IQ difference between MZ twins (Due to environment)	=	IQ difference due to heredity

Arthur R. Jensen, an American psychologist, has gathered together similar results from several studies. In 1969, he published a paper which suggested that, within the white populations of the USA and Great Britain, the differences in IQ scores were caused 80 per cent by genetic factors and 20 per cent by environmental factors. However, an important point must be made here. Jensen's figures are meant to indicate the effects of genetics and environment on the differences in IQ scores for a whole population, not for individuals, so that the 80:20 ratio is probably not actually true of any particular individuals: it is a figure which can be applied only to the populations from which it is obtained. The 80 per cent figure, which is termed the *heritability estimate*, estimates the amount of difference between the IQs of individuals which is caused by genetics; it must be remembered that it does not apply to the total amount of an individual's IQ which is determined by heredity.

Unfortunately the Burt results cannot be relied on, as Burt is believed to have made some serious mistakes in the production of his figures. The Newman, Freeman and Holzinger studies also suffer from defects. When the results are examined more closely it is evident that the monozygotic or MZ twins' different environments were not very different after all. Even though they were raised separately, it appears that there were strong similarities in the type and length of their schooling, in their types of family, and so on. Part of this bias seems to have arisen from the way in which Newman, Freeman and Holzinger obtained their MZ twins. They asked for volunteers by letter, and may have rejected many genuine pairs of MZ twins who appeared to be very different, perhaps believing that too large a difference meant that they were not true MZ twins. Consequently it could be that their sample of MZ twins is biased towards those who were similar.

In order to obtain a heritability estimate Jensen had to provide data by the opposite method too – that of holding the environment constant. He did this, he claims, by comparing people in similar social classes on the assumption that similar social class meant similar environment. Nobody can yet prove that this is not so; we do not yet know enough about the effects of the environment to be certain which factors are important in IQ, but there is considerable doubt that using social class as a yardstick is a sufficiently sophisticated way of ensuring that the environment is constant. To an extent, Jensen's 80 per cent heritability estimate must therefore remain in question.

The Race and IQ Debate

Jensen went still further in his investigations, to argue that in the USA negroes scored, on average, 15 points lower in IQ tests than whites; that the heritability estimate for the white population was 80 per cent; and that therefore 80 per cent of the 15 points difference in IQ between negroes and whites was caused by genetic factors. Not surprisingly, this research caused tremendous argument within psychology. We do not have the space here to deal with the cases for and against Jensen's argument, except to describe a criticism which Hebb put forward against this theory.

Suppose we kept all baby boys in barrels from birth and fed them through the bung-holes until they were mature. If we then tested their IQs and compared them with the IQs of the girls who were reared normally, we should probably find that the girls' IQs were much higher than those of the boys. Because all the boys had been brought up in identical environments, any differences in their IQs should be caused by genetic factors. Could we then say that the boys were less intelligent than the girls, and therefore that, because the differences among the boys' IQs were largely created by genetic factors, these differences between boys and girls were also caused by genetics? Of course not. Firstly we would be comparing IQs, not intelligence as a whole. Also we could not compare the role of heredity in determining the boys' and girls' IQs unless both groups had been reared in identical environments.

If we apply this analogy to the race and IQ debate, we cannot compare the effects of genetics in the determination of negroes' and whites' IQs unless we are sure that they have been brought up in identical environments. Jensen claimed that because he compared middle-class negroes with middle-class whites, and working-class negroes with working-class whites, he had held the environmental variable constant. However, as we have seen, this control may not have been sufficient, or of the right kind.

Leo Kamin, one of Jensen's most vociferous opponents, argues that, whatever the heritability estimate for IQ within a population, the important thing to be considered is which environmental variables affect IQ and how. Remember that genetic and environmental factors interact in development. The example of phenylketonuria mentioned in chapter 3 suggests one of the types of interaction involved: although PKU is a genetic defect, its effects – brain damage as a result of failure to break down phenylalanine – can be overcome by manipulating the environment, in other words by giving food which does not contain phenylalanine. Another example of the interaction of genetic and environmental factors is provided by the markings on Siamese cats. The dark markings on their faces, paws and tails are genetically determined. However, this genetic determination in effect acts as an instruction which causes the hair on the cooler parts of the cat's body to grow darker than the hair on warmer areas.

Thus Siamese cats who are raised until mature in warm climates have markings which are much lighter than traditional Siamese markings.

Genetic instructions, then, seem to provoke the organism to make certain types of response to its environment; change the environment and the genetic instructions will prompt different effects in behaviour or development, as in the cases outlined above. What, then, is a good environment for the development of intelligent behaviour?

What is a 'Good' Environment?

Because it is wrong to assume that intelligence is a thing we possess, it is equally wrong to assume that, like hair- or eye-colour, intelligence has only a few genes as its foundation. This is simply not the case; it is far more probable that many hundreds or even thousands of genes are involved. Thus it may happen that a deliberate alteration in the environment designed to improve the development of behaviour associated with the activity of one group of genes may hinder the development of behaviour associated with the activity of a different group. Figure 40 is an oversimplified illustration of how this might happen if we devised a specialized environment to assist the development of a physical structure. Appropriate stimulation could be provided so that the genetic potential for various aspects of physical development was fully realized.

Figure 40. Effects of One Type of Environment on Different Genes

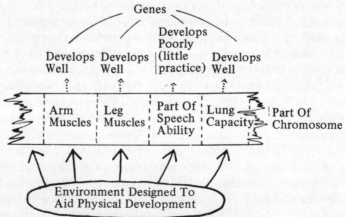

Physical development might progress superbly, but meanwhile, because the environment has been changed in this way, other areas of development might be under-stimulated, and might not develop as well as they would have done in the original environment. So with any change in environment we may at once gain something and lose something somewhere else. It is not enough to recommend a 'good' environment for the development of intelligence. What does 'good environment' mean? There is no one particular type of environment which is 'best' for the development of intelligence.

We have suggested that intelligence is not a single ability; it is more likely the result of the interaction of many different abilities, each with many genes as its blueprint, and each perhaps affected by many different environmental variables. In these circumstances selecting a 'good' environment becomes very difficult indeed: we have to identify which ability we wish to improve, and then isolate those environmental variables which both help that development and do not hinder the development of other abilities.

We now turn to examples of procedures in this field of study. One obvious need for a developing human being is food, and in particular protein, which is necessary to build brain cells. If an adult is starving to death the last area of the body to lose weight is the brain; any other organ will be sacrificed first. But in babies this is not the case: if during the period of brain development the baby is deprived of protein, the brain suffers along with the rest of the body. Although the genetic potential for development might exist, the material with which the body's structures can be built is absent, so that it does not develop properly. J. Cravioto, in studies of protein- and stimulation-deprived children in Mexico, has found that such children show impairment not only of intellectual functions but also of physical development. Moreover, even such simple forms of behaviour as co-ordination between hand and eye – in catching a ball, for example – are affected adversely. Studies are continuing now to attempt to distinguish more clearly between the effects of protein deficiency and stimulation deficiency. Early results suggest that both factors can have separate detrimental effects on the development of intelligence.

At the University of California M.R. Rosenzweig and D. Krech have devised experiments to investigate the effects of a lack of environmental stimulation on normally fed rats. Rats reared with several other litter-mates in a stimulating environment – with treadwheels, ladders, swings, roundabouts, and daily changes in these toys

– showed marked differences in both brain structure and behaviour compared with litter-mates who were reared in an unstimulating environment with one rat to each sound-proofed cage and no toys. The differences were that 'enriched' rats showed a significantly larger brain size with more transmitter molecules – in other words, larger and more active brains – than the 'deprived' group, and that 'enriched' rats were significantly better at solving discrimination-learning tasks than were 'deprived' rats. A stimulating environment, then, seems to help the intellectual development of rats. Hebb's daughter reared rats as household pets, and these animals performed significantly better on maze-learning tasks than litter-mates housed in normal rat cages who were not treated as pets.

Steven Rose of the Open University goes one stage further. Not only can a protein- and stimulation-deprived infancy affect a person's intellectual development but it may also affect the intellectual development of his children and perhaps even of his grandchildren. Malnutrition in a female rat in infancy, for example, may affect her physical and behavioural development: her womb may not develop properly, and she may not develop normal patterns of rat behaviour. Even if she is well fed in later life, the conditions in her womb and her maternal behaviour may be sub-standard, so that the offspring which she rears will themselves be in a deprived environment. This *transgenerational transmission* – so called because it can affect the animal's development before birth – looks like a genetic effect but is in fact an environmental effect. Rose believes that this same process may occur in humans and can be a contributor to the apparently genetic factor in the development of intelligence.

Conversely, however, it is very difficult to pinpoint specific environmental factors which will improve intelligence, because any one environmental alteration may help the development of some intellectual abilities but hinder the development of others; also the timing of the stimulation is crucial (see Sensitive Periods, page 129). Any 'good' environment, therefore, may only be good if it occurs at a particular time in development. It seems that the only basic rule which can be applied is therefore something like, 'As varied and stimulating an environment as possible, as early as possible.'

Thus nobody knows the answers to the nature/nurture debate on intelligence, and there are doubts about whether it is even a valid debate. We still know very little about intelligent behaviour and the factors which affect it.

Summary

1 Intelligence is not a 'thing': it may be a whole number of different abilities, but should best be regarded as a descriptive term, used of behaviour which is appropriate to the environment.

2 Psychologists use the Intelligence Quotient (IQ) as the operational definition of intelligence; this indicates how well an individual compares with others in tests involving logical thinking.

3 It is not possible to find out whether genetics or environment is the major influence on an individual's IQ, but we can try to find out how much they cause differences in IQ.

4 Twin studies are the major research tool for this, but there are severe practical difficulties in carrying them out which make their results rather unreliable.

5 Probably no universal perfect environment exists to help the development of intelligence, because it is not a single ability. Varied stimulation, as early as possible, seems the best recommendation at present.

Chapter 8

Maturation

Psychologists are concerned with how behaviour develops, and we assume that the organism's behaviour enables it to adapt successfully to its environment. Heim's definition of intelligence, and Piaget's and Bruner's descriptions of the functions of intellectual development, stress this point. The term 'development' is thus a very broad one referring to the process whereby as an organism becomes older it becomes more successful in coping with its environment.

Many years have passed in discussion of the fruitless question, what causes development – heredity or environment? Psychologists, as we have seen, used to be split into two traditional opposing camps – those who believed that changes in an organism's behaviour were due to learning, the empiricists, and those who believed that this adaptation was genetically determined, the nativists; but we now assume that both views are justified.

We have already looked at learning as an explanation of changes in behaviour, so now it is time to look at part of the opposing explanation – maturation, including the concepts of Critical and Sensitive Periods. Piaget's theory of intellectual development, for example (see page 95) is a maturational theory. He accepts that environmental factors can alter the rate at which an individual goes through the stages, but it cannot affect the sequence of those stages – sensorimotor, pre-operational, concrete operational and formal operational.

This idea that the genes determine at least the sequence of development receives support from studies of physiological development. For example, a human embryo develops in a fixed sequence: head and tail ends develop first by the eighteenth day, followed at about one month by heart, mouth, intestines and liver. By weeks eight to nine the face, mouth, eyes, ears, arms and legs have developed, although hands and feet are not yet fully formed.

The work of J.M. Tanner on the development of height similarly suggests that after birth, genetic factors are important. For example, in 1962 he found that if an environmental factor such as illness slows down the rate of growth of a child, the growth rate accelerates faster than normal when the illness disappears, as if to catch up in fulfilling its genetic potential.

This genetic control over the sequence of development, or maturation, therefore seems to be a reasonable explanation of physical development. But how much evidence is there that it plays a significant role in the development of behaviour?

Some Studies of the Maturation of Behaviour

Physical structure can be maturationally developed; it can also determine behaviour. For example, humans have no apparent genetic blueprint for wings, so therefore no human can fly unaided. The possession of the physical structure of wings thus enables the corresponding behaviour, flying, to occur. The maturation of physical structure may therefore influence the development of behaviour. It is certain that learning is also involved in any form of development, but in the following studies it is surprising to discover how little learning seems to be involved.

An experiment by L. Carmichael in 1926 brings out this point. A large group of newt tadpoles was allowed to develop until they were just about to start swimming. The group was then split into two, one half of which was anaesthetized while the other half was not treated but kept as the control group and allowed to develop normally. When the control group had been swimming for about five days – by which time their swimming behaviour had fully developed – the anaesthetic was removed from the other group.

Carmichael found that within thirty minutes the anaesthetized tadpoles were swimming, although the anaesthetic solution in the water had prevented them from practising swimming movements until then. Surely their behaviour must therefore be maturational. To make sure that they had not practised as the anaesthetic wore off, Carmichael then anaesthetized the control group and afterwards removed the anaesthetic. Because these could already swim the time they took to recover would not include any practice time the other group might have needed before it could swim. If they had recovered faster, this would have meant that the group first anaesthetized had practised, but in fact the second group also took thirty minutes to recover. Tadpoles' swimming behaviour thus seems to be maturationally determined. It should however be noted here that in 1941 A. Fromme tried to repeat Carmichael's experiment and that his tested group also swam after thirty minutes, but not as well as the control group.

Squirrels bury nuts in autumn, often at the base of trees or large boulders. They scratch a hole in the ground with their forepaws and drop the nut in the hole. Then the nut is rammed into place with the snout, covered up with soil, and the soil stamped down by the forepaws. Eibl-Eibesfeldt reared squirrels in a laboratory, on a liquid diet and in cages with a bare floor. They were well fed, and thus did not need to hoard nuts for the winter. When the animals raised in these conditions were mature, they were given a supply of nuts and observed. First they ate until they were full. Then they took nuts over to a corner of the room, and deposited them there. They then pushed the nuts into the corner with their snouts and made covering and stamping-down movements even though there was no soil. These animals had never before had the materials with which to practise this form of behaviour, neither had they been allowed to see other squirrels doing it. Therefore, Eibl-Eibesfeldt argues, it must be genetically determined; they could not have learnt it.

J.P. Scott and J.L. Fuller experimented to see whether animals could be bred for particular types of behaviour. Several different strains of dog such as terriers and beagles were pure-bred. They were isolated from their mothers as soon as possible, after approximately twenty-one days, and their sensory, motor, and social behaviours were observed. Clear differences were noticed between breeds. Terriers, for example, even when reared in isolation, rushed around far more than beagles also reared in isolation.

By cross-breeding, Scott and Fuller investigated how stable these behaviours were. For example, if in a movement test a terrier scored 75 and a beagle 35 out of a possible 100, what would a terribeagle or cross-breed score? If the behaviour were genetically determined, because each parent contributes half its genes to the puppy, one would expect the terribeagle to score half-way between the beagle and the terrier, a score of around 55. This is broadly what Scott and Fuller found.

The behaviour of some species therefore seems to be largely genetically determined. But Carmichael, Eibl-Eibesfeldt and Scott and Fuller were all using animals in their experiments. Is there any evidence for the maturation of behaviour in humans? A. Gesell carried out some exhaustive observations of the ways in which babies' motor behaviour develops. In all the babies he studied the development of new types of movement progressed as shown in figure 41.

Figure 41. Gesell's 'Directions of Development'

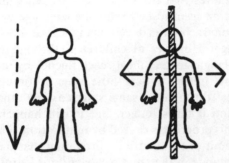

Cephalo-Caudal Direction Of Development (top parts of body develop earlier than lower parts 'Head-to-tail' direction of development)

Proximo-Distal Direction Of Development (centre parts of body develop earlier than outer parts 'Near-far' direction of development)

Although different babies developed the same types of movement at different times, they all did so in the same general sequence. In other words, development had a maturational basis.

Gesell and W. R. Thompson gave one of a pair of MZ twins practice in climbing stairs, while the other twin was deprived of this opportunity. When the trained twin had reached a high level of ability in stair-climbing the other was allowed to try. She reached an equal level of skill but in a much shorter time. Although she may have had a chance previously to practise movements similar to those used in stair-climbing she had not been able to combine them. Therefore the main reason why she learnt faster than the trained twin must have been that she had matured.

Dennis and Dennis investigated a situation in children which was a close parallel to Carmichael's tadpole experiment. Hopi Indian children are kept strapped to their mothers' backs on a cradle board until the age of about six months. Consequently they do not have the opportunity to crawl around on their own or to practise walking in any way. If walking were a learnt ability we should expect these children to walk later than children who were allowed to crawl first. In fact, however, Dennis and Dennis found no difference in the age at which walking began, which thus suggests that practice is not very important; their study illustrates that development of walking ability is determined by maturation.

E.H. Lenneberg, as a result of his studies of language development in children, believes that the sequences through which speech develops in children seem to be fixed. The language we speak is not itself maturational: children develop language as a result of hearing adults speaking it. However, all children go through the same stages in developing language, and most reach fluency by the age of four. No matter how much or how little speech stimulation a child receives, he goes through the same stages as any other child. With little stimulation it takes longer, but it still happens. Lenneberg believes that this progress is caused by maturation. The main factor is not the amount of stimulation – providing that there is some at least – but a change in the child's capacity for learning from such stimulation. The ability to learn would thus appear to be maturational.

In conclusion then, there does seem to be some evidence that maturation plays a part in development; but the preceding evidence in the results of animal studies is much more clear-cut than that in studies of humans. This may be because it is possible to perform more carefully controlled experiments on animals than on humans; but it could also mean that lower down the evolutionary scale more of an animal's behaviour is genetically determined. In insects, fairly low on the scale, most behaviour seems determined genetically, including some very complex kinds of behaviour. Ducks, further up, have some genetically determined behaviour, of which part is fairly complex, for example displays in courtship. Monkeys – near the top of the evolutionary scale – apparently show little genetically determined behaviour, although some simple kinds of behaviour, such as arousal, may be largely genetically determined. At the top of the tree, humans appear to have very little genetically determined behaviour or, according to extreme empiricists, no completely or largely genetically determined behaviour at all.

Critical and Sensitive Periods

The 'maturation' which we have discussed so far is an overall term, referring to a genetically determined sequence of development. However, there are certain types of maturation processes which are different from 'pure' maturation; these special types are termed *Critical* and *Sensitive Periods*, CP and SP. Note that Critical and Sensitive Periods are the same thing; they both describe the same type of maturation, although today the term 'sensitive' is preferred to 'critical' for reasons which will be discussed below. Note also that a CP or SP always applies to the development of a particular form of behaviour. We talk about a CP or SP in the development of binocular vision, or a CP or SP in imprinting, which will be explained in the following paragraph. It may be that each form of behaviour has its own CP or SP, and each of these may occur at a different time.

Experimental Evidence for the CP/SP

The 'classic' demonstration of a CP/SP in behaviour was performed by Konrad Lorenz, the Austrian ethologist. ('Ethology' is the study of animals' behaviour in their natural surroundings.) Lorenz demonstrated a form of behaviour known as *imprinting* in greylag geese. Imprinting behaviour consists of two main parts:

1 At a certain time after hatching the gosling will start to follow the first conspicuous object it sees.

2 After following this object for a period of time – often several hours – the gosling will develop an attachment to the object, and regard it as its guardian; in other words, it imprints on it.

Under normal circumstances this system works well. Goslings are mobile shortly after hatching but are still relatively helpless; by attaching themselves to an adult they ensure their own protection. Lorenz believes that this tendency to follow the first conspicuous object is genetically determined. The gosling does not innately recognize its mother, but because it follows her it learns to recognize her.

Lorenz's experiment went as follows. He took a large clutch of goose eggs and kept them until they were about to hatch out. Half the eggs were then placed under a goose mother while Lorenz kept the other half beside him for several hours. When all the goslings had hatched and dried out, the one group followed the goose but Lorenz's goslings followed him. To check that this was not just chance, Lorenz put all the goslings together under an upturned box and allowed them to mix. When the box was removed the two groups separated to go to their respective guardians – half to the goose, half to Lorenz. The genetic instructions in the gosling's make-up must therefore prompt it to follow the first conspicuous object it sees. That object may be the mother goose; but Lorenz and other researchers induced goslings to imprint on many different objects including boxes, balls and plastic watering-cans.

However, these genetic instructions are not active immediately after hatching; there seems to be a Critical Period during which imprinting can occur. Thus in 1958 E.H. Hess showed that although the imprinting response could occur as early as 1 hour after hatching the strongest responses occurred between 12 and 17 hours after hatching, and that after 32 hours the response was unlikely to occur at all.

Figure 42. Simplified Graph Showing Times of Critical Period for Imprinting

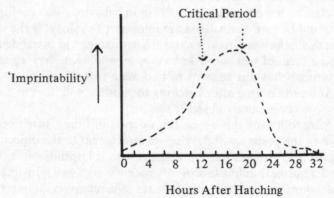

Goslings older than about 20 hours are very difficult to imprint. Lorenz and Hess believe that this is clear evidence for a Critical Period. The appearance of this 'imprintability' appears to be genetically determined. During the CP, if there is a suitable environmental stimulus, imprinting occurs. But they also believe that the disappearance of 'imprintability' is genetically determined, and occurs between 20 and 32 hours after hatching. Thus even if there is a correct stimulus, if it occurs after the genes have switched off the imprintability, imprinting cannot occur. From Hess's results then, the phenomenon occurs between 9 and 12 hours, and disappears again at about 20 hours after hatching. The optimum time for imprinting appears to be 16 hours after hatching.

Not only does there seem to be a Critical Period for imprinting, but once it has occurred Lorenz and Hess believe that it is not changeable. Once a gosling has imprinted on an object or model, it cannot be induced to imprint on anything else: once the duckling has imprinted, the genes switch off the 'imprintability' by switching on avoidance responses in its place; as soon as the gosling has imprinted on one model, it thereafter avoids other models.

However, other researchers do not accept that the Critical Period is in fact critical. W. Sluckin (1961) and P.P.G. Bateson (1964) found that if ducklings are kept away from other ducklings, in social isolation, the imprinting period can be extended well beyond 20 hours. P. Guiton (1958) found that chicks kept in an unstimulated environment – particularly one lacking in visual stimulation – were able to imprint well after the end of the Critical Period. If the animal's experience can alter the length of the period of 'imprintability', the instruction for the disappearance of the phenomenon cannot be all genetic. Therefore Sluckin coined the term 'Sensitive Period', because although the appearance of 'imprintability' may be genetically determined, the animal's experience – its environment – can affect how long it lasts.

Lorenz believes that the model on which an animal imprints influences the animal's sexual preference when mature; for example, a gosling which imprinted on a farmyard hen, when mature, would regard itself as a hen, and try to mate with other hens.

Imprinting, though, has been found to be reversible. Guiton found that ducklings imprinted on chickens in farmyards tried to mate with other ducks when mature. He conducted a laboratory investigation in which ducklings were imprinted on a pair of yellow rubber gloves, and were much later gradually introduced to other ducks. They showed normal sexual preferences, which demonstrates that imprinting, once it has occurred, can be changed. For these reasons the term 'Sensitive Period' is preferred to 'Critical Period'.

Following on from the work of Lorenz, Harlow believed that in higher animals – monkeys of the macaque variety – imprinting leads to the development of an affectionate bond between the infant monkey and its mother.

Empiricists would argue that because the mother feeds the infant, the infant becomes attached to her; such affectionate behaviour is reinforced by the food. Harlow tested this idea by using two mother-surrogates or substitutes, one of which was made of wire and contained the food bottle while the other was covered with terry-towelling cloth – rather like the mother's fur – and did not provide food. Behaviourists would argue that the infant would spend most time with the wire-covered mother, because 'she' supplied food. In fact the infants preferred the cloth-covered mother; it was also noticeable that monkeys reared with the cloth mother showed much more exploratory behaviour than those reared with the wire-covered mother. These latter showed strange behaviour; they would only rarely embrace the wire mother, and most of the time stayed a short distance away, seeming very timid and clutching and rocking themselves for long periods of time. When both cloth- and wire-reared infants were, at maturity, placed with other monkeys it was found that they were largely inefficient mothers: they ignored or mistreated their own offspring (see transgenerational transmission, page 122).

Harlow believed that the preference for the cloth-covered mother showed an innate preference – possibly for the feel of monkey-fur rather than for the mother herself. In young monkeys such behaviour would have survival value: their mothers move around a lot, and this preference would keep them with their mothers, and therefore in safety.

In 1970 R.A. Hinde found that even brief separations of the infant from its true mother can produce long-lasting detrimental effects: the baby alternates between periods of great maternal contact and periods when it rejects the mother. Such effects were found by Hinde to continue for as long as two years after a brief separation. Thus, if an infant monkey is deprived of its mother in infancy it cannot form an affection bond with her. Harlow believed that there is a Critical Period for the development of this bond, and that this Critical Period is roughly from birth to eight months. Infants reared in isolation for more than eight months were unable to form strong bonds with a mother when they were introduced to her and showed no distress if she was parted from them.

Human infants take longer to develop than monkeys, but Harlow believed that the same principles still apply, except that the Critical Period for humans is up to about three years old. Maternal deprivation in infancy can therefore have severe effects on later development.

Maternal Deprivation

Our consideration of the nature/nurture debates on perception and intelligence has shown that severe deprivation can have very marked long-term effects on animals. Riesen's work with perceptually deprived chimpanzees and Held and Hein's work using the kitten carousel both demonstrate that severe and permanent impairment occurs as a result of perceptual deprivation. Harlow's article 'Love in Infant Monkeys' (*Scientific American*, 200 vi (1959) pp. 68–74) describes how monkeys who had been totally isolated from other members of their own species were unable to form affection bonds with their biological mothers or with any other monkey; they showed gross and persistent impairment of social and sexual behaviour.

On the other hand the provision of stimulation in infancy, as we have seen, seems to have beneficial effects. S. Levine raised rats from infancy and handled, petted and stroked half the group, while the other half, the control group, was not handled. The handled rats showed earlier eye-opening, less emotionality – demonstrated by showing less fear in a new situation – and earlier maturation than the control group. The parallels with the work of Rosenzweig on 'enriched' and deprived rats are easily seen: stimulation aids development.

In 1949 R. Melzack and T.H. Scott raised Scots terriers in isolation after weaning them from their mothers. They found two main effects. The dogs reared in isolation were far more excitable and emotional than a control group of normally reared litter-mates. Secondly, probably as a result of this excitability, they were far less able to learn avoidance responses; it was as if they had been so deprived of stimulation that any stimulation, even if painful, was welcome. Normal scotties would avoid the model car which gave them an electric shock after having 5 or 6 shocks. Isolated scotties accepted an average of 23 shocks before they would avoid the car; it was also observed that their perception of pain was different: they seemed less affected by it. One dog was seen to bang into walls, pipes and other obstacles, 30 times within an hour, but did not appear to show any pain.

In 1951 a paper for the World Health Organization by John Bowlby suggested that, particularly in humans, maternal deprivation could be a major cause of many social, emotional and intellectual disorders: '... mother love in infancy and childhood is as important for mental health as are vitamins and proteins for physical health' ('Maternal Care and Mental Health', 1951).

Following up Harlow's experiments described on page 132, Bowlby believed that if a child was not permitted to form an affection bond with its mother it would develop *affectionless psychopathy* – an inability to feel much emotion for anybody else and a lack of interest in anybody else's welfare. He also believed that children who had been deprived of a mother or mother-surrogate were far more likely to show delinquent behaviour later in life. Many people have assumed that in order to prevent these tragic situations full-time mothering is essential, but Bowlby never said this. He simply believed that there must be someone available with whom the child can form an affection bond, but the person need not be the mother.

Nevertheless the findings of Bowlby and other researchers all seem to point to the conclusion that lack of a mother or mother-substitute can lead to social, intellectual and general developmental impairment. We shall summarize some of the best-known findings. In a study of forty-four juvenile thieves Bowlby found that most of them had suffered separation from their mothers for more than six months in their first five years of life. He also found that children who were maternally deprived were unable to form true affection bonds with others, demanding attention but giving little in return. In 1945 R.A. Spitz observed that maternally deprived children frequently showed apathy, slow development and general depression. In 1963 R.G. Patton showed that maternally deprived children often did not develop physically, and were undersized compared to normally reared children. In 1943 W. Goldfarb found that such children when raised in institutions were often retarded in their intellectual and linguistic development. In 1970 J.I. Douglas studied children who suffered stress during their first four years of life, particularly with hospitalization; they were liable to fairly persistent bed-wetting or *enuresis* for several years.

All the above behaviour problems have thus at some time been lumped together under the heading 'caused by maternal deprivation'. But we shall now turn to an examination of each of these problems to determine whether it is certain that maternal deprivation is the cause and to investigate alternative explanations.

Delinquency

Bowlby's original study of forty-four juvenile thieves has been much criticized because his was a biased sample. He found that most of them had suffered from maternal deprivation, and assumed that maternal deprivation must therefore cause delinquency. But he did not have a control group of forty-four non-delinquent children to enable him to ascertain how many non-delinquents had suffered maternal deprivation. In 1961 L.J. Yarrow confirmed that there is quite a high positive correlation between broken homes and delinquency. However, the fact that two things correlate highly does not mean that one need cause the other: a third factor may cause both.

Broken homes often mean separation of a child from his mother, but not all broken homes lead to delinquency; it apparently depends on the type of break-up. Death of a parent, which obviously disturbs home life, does not seem to lead to delinquency, while domestic upheaval as a result of parental separation or divorce often does. (Douglas, 1969). Thus it may be that divorce or separation causes delinquency; however, equally divorce, or separation, and delinquency could all be caused by an unstable relationship between parents, or the child's delinquency may be instrumental in the break-up of the home.

In 1965 M.M. Craig showed that families with a high level of internal conflict were those most likely to have delinquent children. Similarly, in 1971 M.L. Rutter found that delinquency and disturbance were found most commonly in children who had left unhappy homes.

In other words, these studies all suffer from the same problem – the difficulty of distinguishing between cause and effect. This makes it far from certain that maternal deprivation causes delinquency.

Affectionless Psychopathy

Bowlby asserted that affectionless psychopathy was caused by maternal deprivation. However, although fourteen of Bowlby's forty-four juvenile delinquents showed affectionless psychopathy most of a group of children separated from their mothers to go into a tuberculosis sanatorium did not. Simple separation does not seem to be a good enough explanation of this behaviour problem.

Maybe Harlow's infant monkeys suggest a line of thought. They seemed to show affectionless characteristics after having been separated from their biological mothers. How might this form of separation differ from simple separation? The most obvious difference was that Harlow's monkeys were not truly deprived of their mothers, because 'deprivation' implies having something and then losing it. Never having something is known as *privation*. Harlow's monkeys therefore suffered from privation, not deprivation. The monkeys had never been allowed to form an affection bond with their mothers and were later unable to do so with anybody. If, however, a child is allowed to form an affection bond with his mother, who then disappears, at least he has had some experience with bond formation. Privation does not permit any such experience.

Thus maternal deprivation cannot be identified as the cause of affectionless behaviour, while privation can. But need it be *maternal* privation? Anna Freud and S. Dann (1951) investigated a group of six children left parentless by Nazi persecution and raised together, first in a series of concentration camps and finally in an English nursery. The children developed strong bonds with each other, because no parents or parent-substitutes were available. The children were all pre-school age at the start of their group life; it was observed that as time went on, although some of the children showed various emotional problems, there was no sign in any of them of the affectionless character investigated by Bowlby. Privation of bond formation with somebody, though not necessarily the mother, thus seems to be the most likely cause of affectionless psychopathy. H.B. Biller (1971) even suggests that bond formation only with the mother may in itself be inadequate; he suggests that in order to be able to form stable relationships with both sexes in adulthood a child needs the opportunity to form bonds with both parents.

Depression

There appear to be two different causes of depression. Spitz found the problem in long-stay hospital patients, and Douglas found fairly rare cases of depression in children of whom one parent had died. Both situations thus seem to lead to the condition, but they do so in different ways.

Spitz found with the first case that separation from both parents and from the home environment could cause general emotional upset. But these effects could be significantly lessened by counteracting the upsetting strangeness of the hospital atmosphere; this could be achieved either by providing interesting playthings (H. Jolly, 1969) – preventing boredom which could aggravate the problem – or by accustoming the child to the hospital before his actual admission, by allowing him to visit it with parents (J. and J. Robertson, 1955). Death of a parent was found by Douglas occasionally to lead to depression in the child, but he further found that the death of either parent, not necessarily the mother, could be the cause.

Again, maternal deprivation is apparently not the major cause of depression.

Dwarfism

Like the other behaviour problems this cannot be solely caused by maternal deprivation. Two main factors seem to be at work here. First, the standard of care for the child, whether given by the mother or not, may be so low that the child is simply not given enough food to eat. Secondly, even though enough food may be offered the child may not eat it because it is emotionally upset. Again this emotional upset may be caused by the lack of someone – not necessarily the mother – with whom to form an affection bond, or it may be caused by poor relationships between the child and parent or guardian – much scolding or spanking, for example.

Retardation of Language and Intellectual Development

Goldfarb asserted that the major cause of slow development was maternal deprivation. He compared the developmental rates of a group of fifteen institutionalized children from the age range ten to fourteen with a group – matched for heredity as far as possible – who were raised in foster homes, all children having been removed from their natural parents at a few months of age. The group kept in the institution were significantly retarded developmentally compared with the other group. However, he had not considered other possible variables, in particular stimulation.

J.B. Garvin (1963), for example, found a gain in IQ of nine points in children going from unstimulating homes into institutions where they received more stimulation. H.M. Skeels (1966) found a similar effect occurring in children who were moved from a non-stimulating orphanage to an institution for the mentally subnormal where they received more stimulation. W. Dennis (1960) surveyed those institutions where children did not appear to gain much intellectually. He found that a 'poor' or non-stimulating institution was one where the children were rarely handled or talked with; where there were few toys or opportunities for play; and where there was a general lack of sensory, motor and linguistic experience for the children.

Perhaps in a way Bowlby was right; children whose mothers reject them are less likely to be receiving the right kinds and amounts of stimulation. But it is the lack of stimulation which seems to be the major cause of retardation, rather than the lack, or severance, of an emotional bond between mother and child.

Enuresis or Bed-wetting

Much of the evidence suggests that prolonged enuresis often occurs in children who have faced a great deal of stress during their first years, up to the age of six. In 1970 J.W.B. Douglas and R.K. Turner investigated the kinds of situation which may lead to stress in the child. Separation from the mother, father and home appears to be just one factor; there are many others. Like delinquency, enuresis was frequently found in children from homes where there was family discord, because discord produces stress. Stress is also obviously present in children who are in hospital for surgical operations, which often lead to discomfort. These children, too, show a high rate of enuresis. Burn and fracture cases, who usually suffer the most pain, also have the highest rate. Again maternal deprivation may be one contributory factor, but it cannot be said to be a major one.

Thus from the above mass of evidence, which is only a tiny proportion of the total evidence available, one finding seems clear: maternal deprivation is not a single, solitary condition. A child can be deprived of its mother by many means – institutionalization, ineffective or inadequate mothering, maternal rejection. The overall name 'maternal deprivation' therefore covers many different conditions. Moreover, the term 'maternal' is misleading. Much of the evidence suggests that it is not just the mother who is important. Particularly in the case of affectionless psychopathy, the child has simply not had the opportunity to form an affection bond with anyone at all. Thus the chance for bond formation to occur would appear to be essential for problem-free development.

This chance however may only exist for a short time. Remember that Harlow's experiment suggested that there was a Sensitive Period for bond formation in monkeys, and that this Sensitive Period began at birth and lasted for about eight months. M.L. Rutter (1972) suggests that something similar may be true of humans, but that the onset and length of the Sensitive Period are different – from five or six months up to three years, approximately. Harlow also showed that motherless monkeys could be 'rehabilitated' to an extent by being reared with groups of normal monkeys. Again the Freud and Dann study suggests that the same may be true for children; if bond formation is a kind of imprinting it is probably reversible. In humans, remember the account of Sluckin and Guiton's work in the last chapter. As yet, however, not enough work has been done to suggest what are the best techniques to use for the benefit of children who have not been able to imprint.

The affectionless psychopathy studies show that 'maternal' is an incorrect term; they also suggest that 'deprivation' is misleading. A child who can form a bond with another person may show emotional upset if the bond is broken, but he will remain able to form other bonds. On the other hand, a child who has never had the chance to form a bond at all will have much more difficulty. Maternal deprivation, then, is not the major cause of behaviour problems. It can be a contributory factor, but even then it may be so closely linked with other circumstances, such as domestic conflict, that it is imposs- ible to show that it alone has had an effect.

Although there are now obvious doubts about it, Bowlby's work has had some beneficial results. It has made us look much more closely at how we rear our children, and has increased our awareness of how early experiences can affect their later development.

Summary

1 Maturation is a genetically determined sequence of development.
2 Animal studies of tadpoles and squirrels suggest that some forms of behaviour may develop in animals without the opportunity to practise; in humans, body growth seems to be caused by maturation.
3 Studies of language development in children suggest that very little stimulation is needed for language to develop; what is more impor- tant is the maturing of the child's ability to learn language.
4 Critical Periods and Sensitive Periods may both be the same thing. They refer to a particular period in the life of an organism during which it is most likely to be affected by certain kinds of environmen- tal stimulation; see Lorenz's work on imprinting in goslings, and Hess's work with ducklings.
5 'Critical Period' suggests that both the time of the appearance and that of the disappearance of this period are genetically determined;

'Sensitive Period' suggests that although the original appearance of the phase may be genetic, once the organism has responded to a particular stimulus its response may be changed by later stimuli. The disappearance of the phase is caused by the animal's learning a response and is not genetically determined. Many psychologists and ethologists now prefer the term 'sensitive' to 'critical'.

6 Bowlby suggested that maternal deprivation, because it broke the affection bond between child and mother, was the major cause of many types of behaviour problem in later life. Maternal deprivation was particularly damaging if it occurred during the Critical or Sensitive Period for bond formation.

7 Other researchers suggest that the terms 'maternal' and 'deprivation' are both incorrect in this context: a child may be able to form an affection bond with anybody, not just his mother. Privation, rather than deprivation, is a more likely cause of behaviour problems.

Chapter 9

Imitation and Identification

The varieties of learning which we have looked at so far – particularly Classical and Operant Conditioning – involve the gradual development of new forms of behaviour. The development of Learning Sets and schemata can obviously accelerate the learning process, but there is another form of learning which can provide useful 'short cuts' in these rather slow processes. This 'short cut' actually takes two forms – *imitation* and *identification.* They both involve copying somebody else's behaviour, but whereas imitation involves the reproduction of the specific acts of other people, identification refers to a practice which occurs over a longer period of time, using certain models – often our parents. We 'imitate' an act, but we 'identify with' models: we tend to adopt their general behaviour, and even to reproduce their likely behaviour in situations where we have not observed them or had a chance to imitate them. The best-known form of identification is *sex-role identification*, where boys copy the masculine role from their fathers, and girls the feminine role from their mothers. It should be fairly obvious that imitation can play an important part in learning; almost any kind of behaviour can be imitated, from general kinds such as aggressiveness and the use of language to more specific examples such as the development of particular skills.

In general, imitation and identification occur in similar circumstances, so the remarks which follow can be taken to apply to both except where specified.

One of the classic experiments demonstrating imitation was performed by A. Bandura. Nursery-school children were allowed to watch an adult performing aggressive acts towards a large rubber doll, such as hitting it with a hammer, kicking it and picking it up and throwing it. The children were then tested individually in a room containing the rubber doll and other toys; the experimenters noted the total amount of aggressive behaviour shown and in particular the amount of aggressive behaviour which was copied from the adult model. The children who had been allowed to see the adult model performed a large number of aggressive acts towards the doll, about a third of these being direct copies of his behaviour. The other children, who had not been allowed to see the adult model, demonstrated notably fewer aggressive responses, and of these actions very few resembled those of the adult model. This suggests that the children who saw the model were copying him, because the behaviour of the control group did not resemble his. Imitation can therefore take place; but this is something most of us already knew from our own experience.

Some Studies of Imitation
It is not enough to observe simply that imitation can take place; we must make some attempt to define under what circumstances it occurs. An experiment by Bandura, D. Ross and S.A. Ross seems to contradict the apparently straightforward explanation of why imitation might occur, namely that we tend to imitate behaviour which we have seen reinforced in somebody else. This has been termed *vicarious reinforcement*: 'What's good enough for him is good enough for me.' This is the explanation that some conditioning theorists or behaviourists would uphold.

Bandura, Ross and Ross tested this idea in the following manner. First the children used as subjects were split into three groups: one group saw a film in which a model behaved in a most bizarre and aggressive way and as a result this model was punished for his behaviour; the second group saw the same aggressive behaviour but this time the model was rewarded; and in the third film nothing at all happened to the model after the aggressive behaviour. Conditioning theorists or behaviourists would say that group two, who saw the aggressive behaviour rewarded, would show the most aggressive behaviour when tested; that the group who saw the model punished would show the least; and that the behaviour of the group whose model was neither rewarded nor punished would be somewhere in between. The actual results of this experiment did not uphold this prediction. Certainly the group of children who observed the punished model behaved less aggressively when they were tested, but there seemed to be no marked difference between the group whose model was rewarded and the group whose model was neither rewarded nor punished. From these results we can say that although the sight of the model being punished seems to have prevented the children's imitation of his behaviour, the sight of the model being rewarded – having his aggressive behaviour reinforced – did not increase the likelihood that the children would imitate him.

Vicarious reinforcement therefore does not increase the likelihood that a child will imitate the model's behaviour. However, Bandura, Ross and Ross went even further. They wanted to ensure that the three groups of children had learnt equal numbers of aggressive acts from the model, because they felt that it might be possible for a child to have learnt something from him but not to show this learning in his actual behaviour. The three groups of children tested earlier were thus replaced as individuals in the test situation and were then themselves given rewards for aggressive behaviour. All three groups showed approximately the same levels of aggression and, more importantly, roughly the same numbers of their aggressive acts were copied from the model. In other words, all three groups must have learnt the model's behaviour equally, because they were all able to demonstrate the same number and type of aggressive acts in the second test. The group whose model was punished had presumably shown less aggressive behaviour than the other two groups in the first test because of the inhibitory effect of having seen the punishment of their model. They had nevertheless learnt as many aggressive acts as the other two groups, and were willing to demonstrate them when rewarded. Thus we have to make an important distinction between learning and performance: an individual may have learnt something by observing a model but may not necessarily show by his behaviour or performance that he has learnt it.

We can increase the extent of a child's imitative behaviour simply by reinforcing it when it occurs; but this does not really help us to understand why we imitate in the first place. Reinforcement is not the cause, because even without it children still imitate. Why should this be? We think that some animals imitate behaviour – parrots and mynah birds, for example – and it may be that this tendency is innate. Could the same thing be true of humans? The question is still undecided but some work by C. V. Trevarthen (1974) suggests that imitation occurs even in two-month-old babies, who copy their mothers' facial expressions. The ability to imitate would obviously have survival value simply because it enables one to learn adaptive behaviour more quickly and efficiently than is possible through trial and error learning or behaviour shaping. Thus although we are still uncertain, it is feasible that there is some kind of innate tendency to imitate, even in humans. Whether there is or not, there are several major factors which affect our imitative behaviour.

Some Studies of Identification

It may be that we learn any novel behaviour we observe. The Bandura, Ross and Ross experiment previously described suggests that we may learn more behaviour than we perform. However, their evidence also seems to suggest that we are more likely to imitate some models than others. Our earliest models are most likely to be members of our own families – parents, brothers and sisters. It has been argued that we have to learn our particular sex role – masculine behaviour in the case of boys, feminine behaviour in the case of girls – and that we can do so by identification with the appropriate parent. However, if this is true it poses a problem: why should a father be preferred for boys' imitative behaviour and a mother for that of girls? If we instead apply the principles of Operant Conditioning to the family situation it seems plausible that by reinforcing masculine behaviour in a boy, both or either of his parents could ensure that he showed masculine behaviour, and that, similarly, feminine behaviour would be developed in a girl. It thus follows that the presence of either parent is sufficient to promote the development of appropriate sex-role behaviour in a child. So, in the case of a woman living without a husband and rearing her son, provided that she has an idea of normal male behaviour she should be able to reinforce any behaviour in her son which corresponds to this idea and non-reinforce any feminine behaviour that the boy might show. According to the Law of Effect we should therefore expect the reinforced masculine responses to be performed more often than the non-reinforced feminine responses. Summarized in table form opposite are the principles by which behaviour – including sex-role behaviour – can be shaped. Remember that behaviour which is reinforced tends to be repeated, while behaviour which is not reinforced tends to extinguish.

Note also the uses of positive and negative reinforcement here: desired behaviour is given positive reinforcement, such as a smile for saying please when asking for something, or negative reinforcement, for example if a child has a temper tantrum he can be shut up in his room and only allowed out again when he calms down and apologizes.

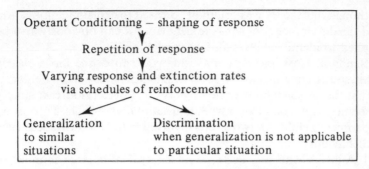

Operant Conditioning — shaping of response

Repetition of response

Varying response and extinction rates
via schedules of reinforcement

Generalization
to similar
situations

Discrimination
when generalization is not applicable
to particular situation

However, there is one substantial criticism of the above process
– which is called *social reinforcement* theory – as the sole explanation
of learning social behaviour; this criticism centres on the concept
of reinforcement. In the case of children rather than animals, praise
and affection are often regarded as far more important than food
as reinforcers in Operant Conditioning. However, simple observation of a child's behaviour and his reactions to praise and affection
from different adults soon reveals that while praise from one adult
may be a very strong reinforcer, praise from a different adult may
not be regarded by the child as reinforcement at all.

Learning or conditioning theorists would argue that such factors
as the amount of previous reinforcement given by a particular adult,
the frequency with which it had been given, and so on, would determine how strong an effect that person's reinforcement would have.
An alternative explanation, both of why some people's praise is a
stronger reinforcer than that of others and of why children do not
imitate or identify with everybody equally, is provided by J.W.M.
Whiting.

According to Whiting boys tend to identify with their fathers and
girls with their mothers because, as Sigmund Freud proposed,
from a very early age boys develop love for their mothers and girls
for their fathers. As a boy cannot possess his mother in the same
way as his father does this creates feelings of envy in the child for
his father's status. Thus the boy begins to copy his father's general
behaviour, presumably in the hope that the more like his father he
becomes, the more likely he is to gain all his mother's love. Both
Freud and Whiting called this process identification. Whiting thus
believes that a boy's envy of his father's status, or *status envy*, is
the main motivator behind his identification with his father.

Although this theory was originally devised to explain identification and the development of sex-role behaviour it can obviously also be applied to identification with any model at all.

Bandura, Ross and Ross have managed to define more clearly what status envy means. It seems that the major factor behind it is that the person who is envied has control over resources; simply to be in possession of resources is usually not enough. Thus in an experiment a child saw two adults involved in the following sequence of behaviour:

1 Adult A who was in apparent control of a large number of expensive and elaborate toys gave some of these to adult B.

2 Adults A and B then performed certain different striking patterns of behaviour which would be easy to recognize in the child if it imitated them.

Then the child's behaviour was observed.

If it is merely possession of the wanted objects which prompts imitative behaviour in the child then we might expect him to imitate the behaviour of both A and B. If, however, it is A's control of resources which is the major motivator then only A's behaviour would be imitated. Observation of the child's behaviour showed that while he imitated some behaviour demonstrated by A and some demonstrated by B, recognizably more of A's behaviour was imitated. This finding suggests that both control of resources and possession of resources act as motivators for imitative behaviour, but that control over resources is probably the more important of the two factors.

We could apply these principles to male sex-role identification:

1 A boy's father is seen by the child to control valuable resources, namely his mother.

2 The boy envies his father's control of this much-desired resource.

3 The boy identifies with his father.

It is evident that a child is liable to find adults' presence, attention or praise reinforcing and will imitate or perhaps identify with them if he can see that they control resources which he himself wants. In conclusion, probably neither Operant Conditioning nor imitation/ identification occurs by itself in any learning situation; the likelihood from these findings is that both processes occur in conjunction with one another.

Summary

1 Imitation means that the individual copies an action performed by the model.

2 Identification involves the individual's copying the general behaviour of another person.

3 Both are 'short cuts' to learning sophisticated behaviour without the need for trial and error learning or behaviour shaping.

4 Bandura found that children will learn to imitate actions from their observation of a model, and that although seeing the model punished affected the extent of their imitative behaviour seeing the model rewarded did not. Rewarding the child for imitative behaviour showed that even when the child had seen the model being punished it had still learnt the behaviour of the model; the punishment observed had simply inhibited the child's performance of it.

5 Sigmund Freud's idea that boys identify with their fathers in order to try to win their mothers' love was modified by Whiting, who believed that boys envied their fathers' status and thus developed an appropriate sex role.

6 Bandura found that control of resources by a model made that model's behaviour more likely to be imitated than the behaviour of a model who did not control resources.

7 These findings can be linked with the Operant Conditioning explanation of sex-role identification; they illustrate that imitation of the behaviour of some people can be more reinforcing than imitation of that of others.

Chapter 10

Child-Rearing Styles

There are many statements made about the treatment of children such as 'Children should be seen and not heard', 'They're only young once, let them enjoy it', 'Spare the rod, spoil the child', 'Children must be protected', 'Children must be allowed independence'. Does it really matter how we rear children as long as their basic requirements of food, water and shelter are met? There are probably as many different ways of bringing up a child as there are children; psychologists, sociologists and anthropologists have tried to group these individual styles into categories and have then studied the relationship between these categories and the development of certain aspects of personality.

It is a fact that the more advanced an animal is, the more helpless are its young, the more dependent and the more affected by experiences in early life. The newborn child is a defenceless object which attempts immediately to gratify any urge – such as the urge to urinate – as soon as it occurs. He must learn to become more self-sufficient in order to survive, and to delay gratification of his urges in order to make his behaviour socially acceptable. The way in which parents help this process of growth inevitably affects a child's development, and as parents differ in the way they fulfil their roles, the later behaviour patterns of their children are also likely to differ.

Parents' treatment of children can vary in the following respects:
1 Their display of love and attention.
2 The type and consistency of their rewards and punishments.
3 The extent to which they give reasons for rules.
4 Their permissiveness.
5 Their control of children's aggression.
6 Their emphasis on behaviour appropriate to the sex roles.
This list is by no means exhaustive, but it includes some of the major categories that have been investigated.

One of the commonest methods of studying the effects of a particular child-rearing style on personality is simply to interview the individual or his parents to find out how he was brought up and to investigate some areas of his personality. If many people with a particular personality were discovered to have been brought up in a way noticeably different from the upbringing of people with a different personality, this would suggest that a certain child-rearing style might have caused the particular aspect of personality in question. However, this method often relies on an individual's memory of how he was brought up, and as we all know, such memories may be distorted. When an individual is asked to look back on his childhood in this way it is called a 'retrospective' study.

'Longitudinal' studies try to overcome the problem of distorted memory by selecting a group of children and following their progress over a number of years. The child-rearing style is thus characterized at the time it is happening, for example by interview or observation; the personality of the child can also be viewed as it is developing.

Both retrospective and longitudinal studies present a problem, which can be exemplified if we study the relationship between physical punishment and aggressive behaviour. It has been found that many aggressive adults have been brought up by parents who used physical punishment as a form of discipline while the parents of many less aggressive adults used far less physical punishment. There are three possible reasons for this:

1 That physical punishment in childhood causes the development of aggressive tendencies.

2 That children who are naturally aggressive frustrate their parents so much that they resort to physical punishment.

3 That some other variable, such as the degree of affection that the parents show to each other, causes both the use of physical punishment and the development of aggressive personality.

Although we often assume that 1 is the explanation of the relationship we cannot be sure that the real reason is not 2 or 3. This is once more the problem of causation: simply establishing a relationship between two variables does not tell us which of these was the cause or, indeed, if either one really did cause the other.

The only way to overcome this problem would be to set up an experiment in which we randomly allocated children to parents who would bring them up in strictly defined ways. If we still found that children brought up with the frequent use of physical punishment were the most aggressive this would be strong evidence that the punishment caused the aggression: the random allocation of children would have ensured that any naturally aggressive subjects would not all have been treated by physical punishment, while factors such as parental relations would have been controlled by having different types of parents using similar methods of upbringing. Unfortunately this sort of research is, of course, impossible to do: who would volunteer to be a subject? However, some experiments can be done on a smaller scale by treating children in different ways for short periods of time and observing the effects (see the study by K. Lewin, R. Lippitt and R. White on page 157). In such experiments we can be sure exactly how the child was treated whereas an interview with parents may give us information simply about how they think the child ought to be treated: theirs will be socially acceptable answers rather than a reliable account.

In addition many researchers have done cross-cultural studies which investigate the differences in child-rearing styles between different peoples of the world. We shall now examine in turn some aspects of personality or behaviour, and the studies of their links with methods of upbringing.

Sex Role
In our culture many people expect boys and girls to behave differently; they expect boys to be more aggressive, competitive and independent than girls. The characteristic behaviour expected of the different sexes, as we have already seen on page 141, is known as sex role. Many people in our society now argue that we ought to break down the sex roles and allow males and females to behave in the same way; others argue that 'Boys will be boys' and that they naturally behave differently from girls. The studies of Margaret Mead suggest that, far from being uniform, there are many variations of the sex roles in different cultures and that the behaviour we can expect from boys or girls depends largely on the way they are treated as children.

Mead studied three groups of people in New Guinea – the Arapesh who live on hillsides; the Mundugumor who live by the riverside; and the Tchambuli who are lakeside dwellers. She found the following differences in the ways in which they were brought up to fulfil the sex roles.

The Arapesh

Both males and females of this tribe are brought up to act in what our society might call a feminine way and in adulthood are gentle, loving and co-operative.

The Mundugumor

Both men and women are self-assertive, arrogant and fierce. They continually quarrel, and Mundugumor mothers have little to do with their children apart from teaching them to taunt their parents.

The Tchambuli

Girls are encouraged to take an interest in the economic activity of the tribe whereas boys are not. The result of this style of child rearing is that men's and women's roles might be seen as the reverse of our traditional roles, the women taking care of trading and food gathering and the men – who are considered sentimental and emotional and not capable of taking serious decisions – spending much of the day in artistic pursuits or gossiping.

Conscience

Some people appear to be able to perform the most horrible atrocities without the slightest pang of guilt; others are worried by their consciences at the smallest dishonesty.

In 1938 D.W. Mackinnon studied the degree to which individuals felt guilt and later related this to the forms of discipline used by their parents. His subjects were set a series of problems to solve, working by themselves in a room that contained answer-books, some of which they were allowed to use and others which they were not. Unknown to the subjects Mackinnon was able to see by means of a two-way mirror that 43 of his 93 subjects cheated.

A few weeks later Mackinnon asked the subjects if they had cheated; 50 per cent of those who had cheated admitted that they had. He found that very few of the cheaters reported feeling guilt or, among the ones who had not confessed, that they would have felt guilty if they had cheated. Most of those who were not cheats said that they would have felt guilty and that they often felt guilt about things they had done or failed to do. In a later enquiry he asked some of the same subjects about their childhood. He found two major types of punishment used by parents – physical punishment, which involved such things as spanking or withdrawal of physical objects such as pocket money; and psychological punishment, which involved, for example, telling the child that he had disappointed his parents or simply becoming less affectionate, looking sad and being quieter than usual. Mackinnon found that most people use both kinds of punishment but employ one more frequently than the other. Most of the children who cheated had parents who favoured physical punishment while the parents of those with stronger consciences used psychological punishment. His results are shown in the following table, which gives the percentage of cheats and non-cheats raised by parents who used physical and psychological punishment respectively.

The Types of Punishment Most Used by Parents

	Physical %	Psychological %
Cheats	78	22
Non-cheats	48	52

Do Mackinnon's results mean that the use of psychological punishment will result in a strong conscience? Let us look at some of the problems:

1 He was dealing with subjects' recall of their childhood experiences; we cannot be sure these were accurate.

2 Even if their recall were accurate it may be that the parents who used psychological punishments were different in other ways from those who used physical punishment and that it was these other differences which caused the children to develop greater or lesser strengths of conscience.

3 We could reverse what seem the cause and the effect: a particular type of punishment might not have caused a certain type of conscience, but instead the children who did not quickly show strong consciences might have exasperated their parents so much that they resorted to physical violence.

It is difficult to overcome the last two problems but the first was solved in a study by R. Sears, E. Maccoby and H. Levin in 1957 who asked mothers about their children's present behaviour rather than requesting adults to recall their childhood experiences. They questioned mothers about the behaviour of their children in situations when they were naughty. Did they lie or admit it, and did they feel guilty? From the mothers' replies they graded each child for his strength of conscience. They also asked the mothers about the way they punished their children for being naughty. This study also showed that children who received physical punishment usually had weaker consciences than those who were punished by psychological means.

If the use of different types of punishment determines the degree to which a child develops conscience, it is important to establish why it should have this effect. Winfred Hill suggests that the techniques of physical and psychological punishment require different responses from the child in order to end the punishment: the psychological type is normally ended when the child has performed some form of symbolic renunciation of his bad behaviour – apologized, promised not to do it again, or promised to make recompense; the physical type generally lasts for a shorter time and requires no such response. Psychological punishment therefore both stops the behaviour of which the parent disapproves and leads the child to perform a gesture of remorse to remove the punishment, while physical punishment simply stops the unacceptable behaviour and may even evoke feelings of resentment without requiring any gesture of remorse. Hill suggests that any form of punishment could lead to strong conscience as long as it induced a symbolic act of renunciation.

The results of studies such as those by Sears and Mackinnon show that children with highly developed consciences usually have parents who make firm moral demands on their children; explain and give reasons for those demands; use psychological rather than physical forms of punishment; and are consistent in their discipline. Children with weak consciences usually have parents who give little explanation for any rules or punishments; use physical or verbally aggressive forms of punishment; are inconsistent in their discipline so that they may punish behaviour simply because they are in a bad mood; and show little affection to each other and the child.

Aggression

Parents differ in their attitudes towards displays of aggression in their children. Studies like that of John and Elizabeth Newson, a longitudinal study of over seven hundred children in Nottingham, show that most parents object to displays of aggression towards themselves, although lower-class parents usually encourage children to 'fight back' and 'stand up for themselves'. As we might expect, studies have shown that the more permissive a parent's attitude towards aggression is, the more aggression is shown by the child.

Sears, Maccoby and Levin showed that another important factor in aggressive behaviour was the extent to which children were punished for it. They studied six-year-old children and found that those who were most punished for aggression were almost as aggressive as the children whose parents were highly permissive; these particular children were usually punished by physical rather than psychological means. Why should a child who is often physically punished be so aggressive? There are several possible interpretations of this finding. Firstly, the parent may provide a model for aggressive behaviour (see page 141): the child sees that when his parents become frustrated they hit out, and he may then decide to imitate them. Such punishment might succeed in preventing aggression towards the parent, which would only result in further punishment, but it might also teach the child that he can get what he wants if he is aggressive towards others, such as weaker children who cannot hurt him. On the other hand the child of a parent who uses psychological methods, distracting his attention from the object of aggression or simply telling him not to hit other people, has to learn to cope with frustration by means other than aggression. Secondly some children may be naturally aggressive and frustrate their parents to such an extent that they have to resort to physical punishment – the causation problem again. The results of a study in 1961 by Bandura, Ross and Ross refute this second explanation. They interviewed the parents of hyper-aggressive boys and argued from their findings that parental rejection and punishment occur before the child shows aggressive tendencies; this suggests that parental behaviour causes a child's aggression rather than the other way round.

When Sears examined the development of the children of the Sears, Maccoby and Levin study six years later, he found that although the children of permissive parents were still aggressive, those of the parents who had used physical punishment to combat aggression were much less aggressive than they had been at the age of six. It seems that by the time a child is twelve, continual physical punishment has been successful in inhibiting violent tendencies; however, the children who had thus been made more peaceable often showed great anxiety about aggression.

Boys usually show more aggression than girls; this may be caused by differences in the way they are treated by their parents. In 1966 Rothbart and Maccoby tape-recorded the spontaneous behaviour of parents towards their children rather than using the more usual interview technique. They found that mothers were usually more permissive towards aggressive acts committed by sons than towards those committed by daughters; fathers tended to be more permissive with daughters. Since it is often the case that the mother spends more time with the child than the father, at least in the early years, these findings may give one explanation of why boys are often more aggressive than girls.

Independence

The new-born baby is a highly dependent creature. By the time we reach adulthood, however, most of us have developed a fair degree of independence; we can make our own decisions and look after ourselves. People do differ, however, in the degree of independence they attain; many seem able to live and take decisions without the help of other people, but some adults find it almost impossible to do so. The degree of independence a child is allowed will depend on two related variables – the child's ability to accept independence and the parent's attitude towards allowing it. These factors interrelate because a child's ability to accept responsibility for his own actions increases to a certain extent with the opportunities he is given for doing so. It is likely to increase further with age and cognitive development. Parents also differ – in the extent to which they allow their children to choose their clothes, go out alone and make decisions such as how to spend their pocket money. They may find it difficult to allow a child independence because they doubt that the child can cope and fear that he may hurt himself. Most parents gradually begin to encourage independence in matters such as dressing, washing and playing alone without constant supervision. However, some find it difficult to allow their children complete independence even when they reach maturity, because this means such a dramatic change in their own life style, after fifteen or sixteen years of being responsible for another individual. The change can be a sign of them growing old or, in the case of those mothers with few other interests, of losing their function in life.

We might expect that if a mother praised her child when he showed independent behaviour and punished him for dependent behaviour she would produce an independent child who could make his own decisions without relying on others, while the child of a mother who consistently rewarded dependent behaviour and rarely encouraged independence would be likely to remain 'tied to his mother's apron strings'. In 1957 Sears, Maccoby and Levin found that rewarding a child for dependency does not necessarily cause him to become dependent; it only has this effect when dependent behaviour is also punished. They found that mothers of the most dependent children sometimes lost their tempers over dependent behaviour and sometimes reacted favourably to it, or they might show irritation when the children turned to them but would eventually give them the attention they required. An example of a situation likely to increase dependency is one where a child cannot decide what to do and so asks his mother; she at first reacts angrily, but when she sees that this upsets the child she sits down with him to play a game. Perhaps the contrast between the punishment and the reward makes the reward seem greater to the child. The mother who sometimes rewards dependent behaviour and sometimes punishes it may therefore simply be giving the child a variable-ratio reinforcement for dependent behaviour; as we have discussed on page 81 this teaches a response which is far less likely to extinguish.

Different types of parent can be graded on a scale according to how much they encourage independent decision making in their children:

Autocratic or Authoritarian	Democratic	Permissive	Laissez-faire
The parent makes all the decisions; the child has no say.	The parent encourages the child to discuss what he wants to do.	The parent allows the child a great deal of freedom of action.	The parent leaves the child to go his own way.

In 1963 G. Elder questioned adolescents about the extent to which their parents explained and gave reasons for any rules that they imposed. He found that *democratic* and *permissive* parents were more likely to do this than *autocratic* parents. He then asked the children questions to test their confidence in their own beliefs and actions, and to gauge their independence in terms of their willingness to solve personal difficulties rather than turn to others. Most confidence and independence was shown by the children of the democratic and the permissive parents, who frequently explained the reasons for their rules, whereas the least confident and independent individuals tended to have autocratic parents who did not give reasons. It may be that autocratic treatment undermines a child's confidence in his own powers of decision making while democratic and permissive attitudes allow a child to practise making his own decisions and to succeed in doing so.

In 1938 K. Lewin, R. Lippitt and R. White performed an experiment to investigate the effects of autocratic, democratic and *laissez-faire* adult behaviour on groups of ten-year-old schoolboys attending after-school clubs. Each club was led by an adult who acted in either an autocratic, democratic or *laissez-faire* manner. The autocratic leaders told the boys what sort of models they were going to make and with whom they would work while the democratic leaders discussed the various possibilities for projects and team work with the boys and allowed them to make their own decisions. The autocratic leaders sometimes praised or blamed boys for their work but unlike the democrats they did not explain their comments; for example, an autocrat might say 'Good boy, Johnny' while a democrat might say in the same situation 'It's very good the way you have managed to make your plane more realistic by including windows'. The democratic leaders joined in with group activities; the autocrats remained aloof from their groups, friendly but impersonal. The *laissez-faire* leaders of course left the boys to their own devices, only offering help when asked to do so – which was infrequent – and offering no praise or blame.

The psychologists found that the boys' behaviour and their attitudes to work differed according to the degree of independence allowed by their particular leaders.

The Autocratic Approach
The boys became aggressive towards each other or simply apathetic. They were submissive in their approaches to the leader, which were often made simply to gain attention. If he left the room the boys stopped work and became disruptive. When frustrated by a problem the boys would blame each other rather than co-operate to solve it.

The Democratic Approach
Relationships between the boys were much better than in the autocratic situations: they showed less aggression and liked each other

more. Approaches to the leader were usually task-related rather than attention-seeking. Although slightly less work was done than with the autocrat, the boys did not stop working when the leader left the room, thus showing that they were more independent of the leader than were the groups with the autocrat. When frustrated by a problem the boys would co-operate to solve it.

The *Laissez-faire* Approach

These groups were chaotic. The boys' relationships were aggressive although not as much as in the autocratic groups. Very little work was done whether the leader was there or not. These groups did not even do enough work to encounter problems related to the task; they simply gave up when the work became in the least way demanding.

Later the children were grouped differently and the leaders were asked to adopt one of the other kinds of approach. The behaviour of the children was thus proved to depend on the style of leadership and not on the particular personalities involved.

The study of Lewin, Lippitt and White had examined the effect on boys of the behaviour of adults other than their parents when these children had already experienced ten years of parental treatment. Thus it must be remembered that the fact that most of the boys preferred democratic leadership may have been because their parents were mostly democratic, while some less independent boys who showed preferences for the autocratic style might equally have been reflecting their parents' style. This study nevertheless suggests the possible effects on children of these three types of leadership when put into practice by parents.

Achievement Motivation

Some people have a great need to succeed in everything they do while others show little interest in achieving anything; thus people are said to differ in the extent to which they display *achievement motivation*. In 1938 D.C. McClelland showed how the 'thematic apperception test' or TAT could be used to measure achievement motivation. The TAT consists of a series of pictures. A subject is asked to take each picture in turn and to write a story about it. Because different people will write different stories it is argued that the differences will be reflections of individual personalities. A typical picture used to test achievement motivation might be that of a boy holding a violin and staring vacantly into space. The tester would look for such things as whether a story deals with getting on in school or a career and whether it involves success; the more it involves these, the greater achievement motivation the subject is thought to have. McClelland argues that if two people have similar abilities but one has greater achievement motivation then he is the one more likely to do well.

In 1953 Marian Winterbottom measured the achievement motivation of children by asking them to tell a story which would expand short sentences given to them, such as 'Two children were running a race when one fell over.' She then interviewed the mothers of children with high and low achievement-motivation scores. Each mother was asked 'At what age did you expect your child to know his way around the city; try new things for himself; succeed in competition; and make his own friends?' She found that the mothers of high scorers had expected these things of their children at an earlier age than the mothers of low scorers. The mothers of children with high achievement motivation usually rewarded the child with physical affection; the mothers of low scorers placed more restrictions on their children, giving many instructions about where they could go, what they could do and with whom they were allowed to play.

A study by B. Rosen and R. D'Andrade in 1959 also showed a relationship between the expectations of parents and the achievement motivation of their sons. With his parents watching, a child was blindfolded and asked to build a tower of building blocks with one hand. His parents were asked how well they thought he would do; it was found that the parents of those with high achievement motivation had higher expectations. Parents also differed in their behaviour while the boys built the towers. The most notable behaviour of parents of children with high achievement motivation was that the mothers tended to encourage their children and to show great pleasure when they succeeded in placing a block. The most notable parental behaviour towards the children with low achievement motivation was that the fathers tended to tell their children what to do and showed disapproval when they failed.

The results of studies like these suggest that the child with high achievement motivation will have been encouraged to be independent and to seek reward while the child with low achievement motivation will have been told what to do and will simply attempt to avoid punishment.

General Styles or Specific Practices?

In the preceding sections we have discussed general styles of child rearing – authoritarian, permissive and so on – rather than specific practices such as toilet-training or breast-feeding. Freud suggested that the way a parent approaches the potty-training of the child may have a lasting effect on the child's personality. Although excessive emphasis on training, and punishment for failure to learn, may lead to signs of anxiety and even to delay in successful training, there is no strong evidence to suggest an effect later in life.

John and Elizabeth Newson argue that the reason for the difficulty in correlating specific practices with later personality is that these practices 'are a good deal less important in the long term than the spirit in which they are carried out'. The study of general styles and philosophies of child rearing is thus likely to be more productive.

In presenting the results of studies on child rearing one is in danger of giving the impression that there is a formula by which to bring up children to be as moral, peaceable, independent and motivated as a parent desires. This formula obviously does not exist; these studies can only scratch the surface of the variables which affect behaviour. Most of the studies we have presented in this chapter supply correlational evidence and thus suffer from the causation problem, despite the convincing pronunciations of the psychologists involved.

We must also beware of accepting at face value the results of interviews with parents and children; there is always the possibility that some of them simply tell us what they think we want to hear rather than describing how they actually behave. Only when we find that the results of independent studies which involve interviews with children, such as Mackinnon's, give similar answers to studies involving interviews with parents, such as those of Sears, Maccoby and Levin, will this give us more confidence in the findings.

Despite such problems these studies do give us some useful insights into the social development of the child.

Summary

1 The relationship between child-rearing style and personality has been studied by retrospective, longitudinal and experimental methods.

2 Major problems include:

(a) Memory problems.

(b) The causation problem.

(c) The problem that parents may be biased to give us 'socially acceptable' responses to our questions about the way they rear their children.

3 Mead showed that sex roles differ according to the ways boys and girls are treated in different cultures.

4 The studies of Mackinnon and of Sears, Maccoby and Levin suggest that strong conscience is a result of:

(a) Firm moral demands on children.

(b) Explanation of those demands.

(c) The use of consistent psychological punishment.

(d) An affectionate family relationship.

5 Sears, Maccoby and Levin showed that aggressive personality increases with parental permissiveness and the use of physical punishment.

6 Parents differ in the degree of independence they allow to their children. The most dependent children usually have parents who both punish and reward dependence.

7 Different types of parent can be graded on a scale according to how much they encourage independent decision making in their child. The scale ranges from the autocratic parent, who makes all the decisions himself, to the democratic and the permissive parent, and finally to the *laissez-faire* parent who takes no responsibility for the child. Lewin, Lippitt and White showed that children were more likely to work on their own if in the charge of a democratic leader rather than of an autocratic one; other differences in this situation included less aggression and greater willingness to co-operate.

8 Winterbottom demonstrated that the level of achievement motivation is highest in children whose parents expect earlier independence. Rosen and D'Andrade found higher expectation and more encouragement in parents of those boys with high achievement motivation.

9 The studies of general styles of rearing – authoritarian, democratic and permissive – appear to be more productive than those on specific practices such as toilet-training, in their contribution to our understanding of the development of adult personality.

Chapter 11

The Development of the Self-Concept

As the individual develops, he becomes more able to cope with his environment. However, in addition to finding out about his environment, he also finds out about himself and develops attitudes towards himself and his behaviour. Such knowledge and attitudes are known as the *self-concept*.

What is the Self-Concept?

Who am I? What am I? The answers I give to these questions constitute my self-concept which consists of:

1 *Self-image*. This part is simply descriptive, for example I am a student, a brother, a squash player, six feet tall, and so on.

2 *Self-esteem*. This part involves an evaluation, an estimation of self-worth, for example I am friendly, reasonably intelligent, and so on.

Piaget (see page 95) tells us that at first the new-born infant does not distinguish between himself and other physical objects, but that during the first six months or so, as he develops ideas about what objects are, he also begins to see himself as different from the rest of his environment. At a fairly early age most children respond to their own names but it is not until about the age of two that they begin to use them to describe themselves. By the age of four most children are obsessed by the idea of 'my' car, 'my' slide, 'my' brother, as though they are extending the idea of self to their possessions. The self-concept probably changes fairly frequently during childhood, but in our culture it often becomes an especial problem during adolescence. This is both the phase when the body changes dramatically, thus changing the self-image, and the time for making decisions about one's personality in order to cope with questions such as career choice.

These problems of self in the years of adolescence are inevitably affected by social environment as well as by the individual's actual capacities. There are four highly related factors which affect the development of the self-concept (M. Argyle, 1969) – the reaction of others; comparison with others; the roles an individual plays; and identification with others.

The Reaction of Others

In 1902 C.H. Cooley argued that by observing the reflection of our behaviour in the responses of others, we learn about ourselves. If students respond well to a teacher's lessons, showing an interest in the subject, this will help him to form an image of himself as a good teacher, whereas if they ignore him and appear bored a very different self-image will be formed.

E. Guthrie (1938) tells a story about one of his female students, a dull, unattractive girl. Some of her class-mates decided to play a joke on her by treating her as though she were the most attractive and interesting girl in college. The students drew lots to decide who should have the unenviable task of asking her out first, second, third and so on. Guthrie noticed that by the time the fifth or sixth boy came to ask her out he did not consider it such a bore; by the end of the term the girl had become an interesting and confident type. She had changed her self-concept because of the reaction of others towards her, which in turn had changed her behaviour; her reflection of a new self-esteem meant that people now really did find her interesting.

Self-concept is built up over a long period of time, and it is unlikely that one unusual reaction from an individual will change it, but if the type of reaction occurs very frequently, or if it is made by *significant others* – people we value such as parents or friends – then this is likely to affect our self-concept. The self-concept can be divided according to different areas of an individual's activity, for example self as an academic, sportsman and socialite; thus the identity of significant others who can affect one's self-concept will depend on which particular aspect is evoking a response. A teacher is more likely to affect the academic self-concept of a person than to have any effect on his social self-concept, on which friends will have more influence. The self-concept is relatively stable because we usually choose friends who regard us in a similar light to that in which we see ourselves; they therefore serve to reinforce our self-concept.

The most significant others for the majority of children are parents; a child is deeply affected by their views of him as intelligent, naughty, quiet, fat, strong and so on. In 1967 S. Coopersmith showed that the way parents treat their children influences their self-esteem. He analysed schoolboys for their degree of self-esteem by combining their own self-evaluation with evaluation by their teachers, and by evaluating the stories they told in response to TAT pictures (see page 158 for details of the TAT). He found the following differences:

Parents of Children with High Self-Esteem	Parents of Children with Low Self-Esteem
More likely to praise child for good behaviour	Less likely to praise child for good behaviour
More democratic	Less democratic
Showed more interest in child	Showed little interest in child
Neither extremely punitive nor permissive	Either punitive or permissive
Punished consistently and promptly	Punished inconsistently
Rarely used withdrawal of love as a punishment	No corresponding findings

Comparison with Others

A great deal of our self-concept depends on how we compare with others. Adults commonly make comparisons between brothers and sisters; an average child might think of himself as a dullard simply because of continual comparison with a highly intelligent brother. We usually prefer to compare ourselves with people who are fairly similar to ourselves: a club cricket player is likely to compare himself with other players in similar clubs rather than with those who play for England or who have just started the game. Thus parts of the self-image may change quite rapidly with a change in social situation, for example a person may think of himself as young when working with older people but suddenly feel old when he changes to a job where his associates are mostly younger than he is.

The Roles an Individual Plays

Each person, as we have said, plays many different roles; in each of these he is expected to act in a particular way. I am expected to act differently in my capacities as a teacher and as a husband. Thus the expectations and experiences connected with different roles are likely to affect the self-concept of the individual.

In 1960 M. Kuhn showed that individuals incorporate more and more roles into their self-concept as they grow up. His subjects were asked to respond to the question 'Who am I?' by making twenty statements. He found that seven-year-olds included only about five statements related to role, while university students included twice this number. Examples of statements relating to role would be: I am a mother, a daughter, a woman, a clerical officer; examples of other types of statement would be: I am lazy, inhibited, careless, attractive.

Identification With Others

When children particularly admire an adult they often try to identify with him (see chapter 9), adopting many of his or her values, beliefs and actions. This process of identification causes the child to feel that he has many of the attributes of the person he admires. A change in self-concept, usually short-lived, can also occur after seeing a particularly dramatic film which brings about an identification with the hero; this rapidly disappears as reality reasserts itself. This process of identification is a possible explanation of Coopersmith's findings that children with high self-esteem usually have parents who also have high self-esteem. Sex roles influence self-concepts and in our society males and females often differ in their characteristic attitudes to qualities such as aggressiveness and competitiveness (see page 155). One of the ways in which a child assumes his or her sex role, and thus develops a self-concept, is by identification with the parent of the same sex.

The Body Image and the Self-Concept

Anorexia nervosa is a condition suffered mainly by teenage girls; it involves a refusal to eat until the sufferer becomes more and more like a skeleton and may die. No one really knows what causes this disorder but such girls seem to have a distorted body image. They see themselves as overweight even when others would regard them as slim. The body image is that part of the self-concept which refers to physical attributes, and it is affected by each of the four factors discussed above. It is particularly affected by ideas about what is beautiful and what is ugly; these concepts vary from culture to culture. The possession of characteristics which approach the so-called 'ideal body' may influence the reactions of others and thus affect self-concept.

During adolescence greater interest in the opposite sex, together with a rapid change in bodily characteristics, leads to an increase in the importance of the body image as part of the self-concept. Body image is probably more important at this stage than at any other. In 1962 F. Arnhoff and E. Damianopoulos showed that twenty-year-olds, just beyond adolescence, had a more definite body image than forty-year-olds. He took photographs of individuals dressed only in shorts and blotted out their facial characteristics; the younger subjects were better at recognizing their own photographs from a group of six than were the forty-year-olds.

Many studies, such as those of A. Jersild in 1952, show that when asked what they do not like about themselves very few adolescents mention their abilities, but about 60 per cent quote some aspect of their physical appearance, and most often facial defects, especially skin complaints. Such dissatisfaction usually reflects physical discrepancies between reality and the ideals often displayed in magazines, television and advertisements.

The idea that physical characteristics are related to personality is not new; people are said to 'look intelligent' or 'shifty-eyed', and red hair is supposed to be a sign of a quick temper. In 1963 A. Hood gave personality tests to a thousand new college students and found only very small differences between individuals of widely different body types. He argued that too much emphasis is placed on the effect of body image on personality.

Studies performed at the University of California suggest that the time at which the adolescent growth-spurt occurs may have an important effect on the self-concept. A boy who matures late will find that his peers start to race ahead of him in size and strength, that their voices change and that they start to grow body hair. Suddenly a boy who has compared favourably with his contemporaries may feel immature in comparison. A similar reaction to their physical changes occurs in girls. In 1950 M. Jones and N. Bayley picked the most advanced and retarded boys from a group of fourteen- to eighteen-year-olds and studied their personalities and the way in which adults and peers reacted to them. They found that in comparison with late maturers, those who matured early were usually seen as more attractive, less childish and less talkative. The early maturers showed more interest in girls at the age of fifteen and were more likely to be popular and hold positions of responsibility. Adults considered the late maturers as more childish and attention-seeking. At the age of seventeen the early maturers were still found to be more self-confident and less dependent; those who had matured late had very strong desires for contact with girls and were more aggressive. In 1963 D. Eichorn did a follow-up study of these subjects at the age of thirty-three, to discover the long-term effects of these differences on their self-concepts. He found that the late maturers were more likely than others to seek aid and encouragement from others, that they were more impulsive and touchy but had greater insight into other people's problems – perhaps owing to their own early experiences of social problems.

In 1958 P. Mussen and M. Jones showed that at the age of seventeen girls who mature early are more self-confident than late maturers, but the difference between late and early maturation in girls does not have as great an effect as in boys.

It is important to point out that the studies described concern boys and girls who are extremely advanced or retarded in maturation. In 1964 D. Weatherly showed that the boys who mature at average age are very similar to those who mature early; it therefore seems to be only late maturation which causes difficulty. The studies of the effects of early and late maturity stress the importance of the comparison of the adolescent with others in the formation of his self-concept. This comparison is made not only by the adolescent himself but also by his parents and peers, whose treatment of him as an adult or a child in turn further affects his self-concept.

Summary

1 Self-concept consists of two main parts – self-image (descriptive) and self-esteem (evaluative).
2 Self-concept develops by the action of four factors:
   (a) The reaction of others.
   (b) Comparison with others.
   (c) The roles an individual plays.
   (d) Identification with others.

168   BEGINNING PSYCHOLOGY

3 Coopersmith showed that the style of child rearing affects the development of self-esteem.
4 Body image plays an important part in the self-concept, especially for adolescents.
5 Late maturation can have a lasting effect on the self-concept of males. It has far less effect on females.

Chapter 12

Non-Verbal Communication or NVC

Human *communication* occurs whenever a piece of information passes from one person to another, whether the message is intentional or not. It was noted in chapter 6 that Bruner argues that linguistic communication acts as an accelerator for intellectual development (see page 103); without communication much human behaviour would be very different.

Verbal communication – speaking and writing – is a very efficient form of communication which allows the transmission of complex information from one person to another. While talking, however, people also communicate on a non-verbal level through posture, facial expression and gestures; communication without some of these ancillaries – as happens in a telephone conversation – may create many difficulties of interpretation and understanding. The basic difference between *verbal* and *non-verbal communication* is that the former makes use of language, using letters, words and sentences in both spoken and written form, whereas the latter does not. Apart from this difference the two forms of communication differ in their capacity for ambiguity and in the extent to which they are voluntary. Usually individuals make their speech clear and unambiguous although they sometimes use ambiguity for special effect, as in jokes for example. With NVC, signals are more often unclear: a particular facial expression might signal either agony or ecstasy. We should assume from studying a photograph of adoring fans at a pop concert that they were in ecstasy because we should know about the situation they were in, but if we were told that they were at a funeral, the same facial expressions might successfully convey a totally different message. NVC must be interpreted in the context of the situation and the combination of all signals from the face and hands, body position and so on, to avoid this ambiguity. On the whole our verbal communication is voluntary; we say what we want to and refrain from saying things we want to hide. Perhaps because we attach so much importance to verbal communication we often give non-verbal signals without realizing it. The student who glances at his watch and yawns during a lesson would probably not say to his teacher that he wishes the lesson would end, but he might well convey the message all the same by unthinkingly using this set of non-verbal signals.

Animals have no known language and hence do not use verbal communication, but they are able to communicate in a non-verbal manner by employing smell, touch, sight and hearing; in humans a great amount of communication occurs on a verbal level but we have not lost our ability to use non-verbal communication, which performs a number of functions. Amongst these, it may replace speech; signal attitudes towards others; signal emotion; and aid verbal communication. Note that non-verbal signals may fulfil any of the above functions at a given time.

Figure 43. Interaction as a Social Skill

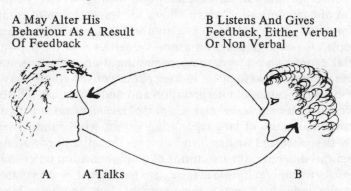

A May Alter His
Behaviour As A Result
Of Feedback

B Listens And Gives
Feedback, Either Verbal
Or Non Verbal

A   A Talks   B

Michael Argyle (1967) sees social interaction in all its forms as a learnt skill. It requires the ability not only to send out messages to other people but also to discover from them how these messages are being received, in other words it requires *feedback*. Thus if A and B are in conversation and A is talking, he is at the same time on the lookout for feedback from B that indicates such things as agreement, understanding, interest and the wish to start talking himself. These signals may take a verbal form: B may say 'Yes, I agree' or 'Let me get a word in', but many of them will be non-verbal – head-nodding, looking at A, smiling and so on. To most of us, these non-verbal signals are so well learnt in childhood that we do not even notice that we are using them. They only become noticeable when something goes wrong, for example if an individual is from a different culture which has different signals or if someone has had a socially isolated childhood.

Methods of Study

The main method of studying NVC has been simple observation, watching people as they interact. When people know they are being watched they often become self-conscious and do not behave as they would normally. To overcome this difficulty many studies have used two-way mirrors so that the researcher can observe without being observed. Increasingly, researchers are using film to record the interactions of their subjects. This has the great advantage that it can be viewed and re-viewed, slowed down and speeded up, to observe elements of behaviour that might be missed within the limitations of a single, normal-speed viewing.

Sometimes people are asked to behave in certain ways in order to study the effect on others, for example increasing or decreasing the number of times a stooge nods his head while listening to a subject to assess the effect on the length of time for which he talks. Other studies have used a role-play procedure: A. Mehrabian (1968) instructed his subjects to talk to a hat-stand as if it were a particular type of person and found that when talking to 'people' supposed to be of higher status they raised their heads.

NVC as a Replacement for Speech

It is important here to distinguish between NVC and some forms of verbal communication that do not use the spoken word. Semaphore is not NVC: because it signals letters, words and sentences it is a form of verbal communication. Communication simply has to use language in some form to be verbal; a book or an essay therefore counts as verbal communication. NVC does not make use of the letters of the alphabet; it signals meaning without spelling words.

NVC can replace verbal communication when the latter is not possible, for example because of distance or noise. The single finger placed vertically over the lips does not require the verbal command 'Be quiet.' We all know how to signal 'Come over here' without using any words. In a car it is not possible to shout to other drivers that we are turning right or left and so we use hand signals or flashing lights.

The meaning of a signal may vary from culture to culture; for example to stick out the tongue, which in Britain is often regarded as an insult, in China is an expression of apology or surprise; in Tibet is a sign of respect; and on the Marquesan Islands means 'no'.

NVC to Signal Attitudes towards Others

An example of the way in which many signals combine to form a communication is the signalling of friendship and intimacy. Argyle argues that the degree of intimacy is signalled by at least four factors – proximity; eye contact; smiling; and personal topics of conversation. Young lovers in conversation will stand very close, perhaps even touching, look into each other's eyes a lot, smile and talk about personal things. Two people who are relative strangers will stand further apart and make less eye contact; their topic of conversation is more likely to be the weather or some other impersonal subject. More intimacy is indicated by an increase in all four factors. However, sometimes external events may cause only one factor to change; for example, in a crowded London tube-train people's proximity increases and yet they are perfect strangers. They must therefore avoid signalling a degree of intimacy which is not there, and do so by decreasing the amount of eye contact that they have with other people. On a crowded tube the best way to do this is by looking up towards the ceiling – hence the location of advertisements on the tube.

If somebody gives inappropriate signals about intimacy this can be very embarrassing; people who have not learnt the 'rules' of NVC and stand too close or make too much eye contact with others may find it difficult to make friends for this reason. Argyle argues that many people may be lonely or have social problems because for some reason they have inadequately learnt the language of NVC. These people may be helped by training.

Although in our culture proximity signals intimacy it is common in parts of Africa and Asia for people in conversation to stand much closer together, even touching each other. When people from different cultures meet they have to cope with these differences.

The pupils of the eyes dilate when we feel happy or when we like something or someone. In 1963 E.H. Hess found that men preferred pictures of girls with dilated pupils to identical pictures in which their pupils were not dilated, even when the men could not say what the difference between the photographs was. This may be because we like people who signal they like us.

How much a listener looks at whoever is addressing him indicates the extent of his interest in what he is hearing; this can influence the amount of talking that the other person does. It is difficult to talk to someone who refuses to look at you. A student once reported that during his school life he had stopped talking to his teachers after class because they would talk to him endlessly. He found, however, that his friends did not have the same problem and he could not understand why. Apparently the reason was that this student continued to look at his teachers while in conversation, which was interpreted as the normal signal to continue. It is actually quite difficult to stop talking while somebody does this. Once his problem was discovered this particular student became adept at stopping conversation by lowering his gaze and looking away.

The type of interest – for example, whether we like or dislike the person – is signalled by facial expression, which can also indicate our emotional state as described below.

NVC to Signal Emotion
I. Eibl-Eibesfeldt argues that many of the facial expressions characteristic of states of emotion such as anger, sadness and happiness are innate and do not need to be learnt, because children who are born both blind and deaf show basically the same facial patterns of laughing, smiling, crying and sulking as do normal children. The top half of the face around the eyes and eyebrows seems particularly important in signalling emotions: the eyebrows are raised in surprise, the brow is furrowed when we are worried.

Facial expression alone is often not enough to give a precise understanding of which emotion is being felt; we need to know more about the context in which the expression is being given. It is for this reason that subjects of experiments often make as many as 40 per cent errors when asked to judge the emotions expressed by faces in photographs. However, H. Schlosberg (1952) showed that subjects were unlikely to mistake contempt for fear, disgust for surprise or happiness for anger; they were much more likely to mistake disgust for contempt, happiness for surprise and fear for anger.

S. Kasl and G. Mahl (1965) have examined the non-verbal aspects of speech itself – not what is being said but the messages that can be understood from how it is being said. As well as signalling such things as class, sex, age, and place of origin, we can also express emotions such as anxiety by the way in which we speak. Errors in speech can also be significant: Kasl and Mahl distinguished between 'ah' errors when the speaker inserts an 'er', 'ah', or 'um', into his sentence and 'non-ah' errors which involve repetition, stuttering and slips of the tongue. 'Ah' errors occur more when a speaker is talking on a subject that he finds difficult; it is as though they give him time to think. 'Non-ah' errors increase with anxiety and can therefore communicate it. We have a fair degree of voluntary control over the muscles of the face and can use it to disguise our feelings, but we seem to be far less successful in concealing our emotions by control of our voice and hands.

NVC as an Aid to Verbal Communication

It was noted earlier in this chapter that when talking on the telephone we emit certain sounds to show that we are still listening, but in face-to-face conversation we are also able to do this by using such signals as head-nods and eye-gaze. In 1967 A. Kendon filmed people in conversation and established different patterns of eye contact in speakers and listeners. The listener spends more time looking at his partner than does the speaker, who starts by looking away from the listener, glancing up from time to time and looking back at the listener at the end of his utterance. Head-nodding and smiling on the part of the listener act as reinforcers, because as we have seen, they increase the length of a speaker's utterances. When the speaker glances up at his partner he not only receives messages to stop or go on but also information which tells him how to continue; a facial expression of doubt, disbelief or boredom is likely to prompt a different response from that prompted by agreement or interest. When speaking on a difficult subject a person looks up less, probably because he needs to attend more to his subject than to its effect on the listener. During these conversations Kendon observed that listeners often mirror the gestures and facial expressions of speakers.

The end of an utterance is often signalled by a change in the positions of the speaker and listener. The power of this gesture as a form of communication can be illustrated by the case of Clever Hans, an 'intelligent' circus horse who appeared to be able to solve arithmetical problems. If Hans was asked to give the answer to the problem 'two plus two' he would strike the ground four times with his hoof. Hans could solve an amazing range of such problems and many believed that he could really think mathematically, but in 1911 A. Pfungst showed that if the questioner hid from Hans's view the horse would go on striking the ground even after he had reached the correct answer. The horse had learnt to stop 'counting' when his questioner made the slight change in posture that we all make when we have received the desired answer and believe that a communication has ended.

In 1967 P. Ekman and W. Friesen argued that cultures and classes differ in the signals they use to accompany conversations; other people may appear rude or difficult to talk to simply for this reason. In emphasizing points in their verbal conversations the Italians use arm gestures far more than do the British. Because Arabs stand much closer, often touching, during conversation, they can make use of changes in position and pressure of touch more effectively than can the British or Germans who stand further apart. Although we do not have a precise translation for NVC, many teachers of language see the need to teach both verbal and non-verbal aspects of communication to their students. Gestures such as head-nodding or -shaking often accompany the words 'yes' or 'no' but even this is not universal. Visitors to Greece may very well have problems since when a Greek says 'no' he raises his head in a way that a Briton could mistake for a 'yes' signal, especially since the Greek word for no, 'ochi', sounds like 'OK'.

Summary

1 For successful social interaction an individual needs feedback about the effects he is having on others. This feedback may take the form of verbal or non-verbal communication.

2 Although some facial expressions of emotion may be innate, much of NVC is learnt. Differences in NVC shown by people of different cultures or those who have not learnt adequate non-verbal skills may cause difficulties and embarrassment in interaction.

3 NVC may replace speech, signal interpersonal attitudes, express emotion or simply aid verbal communication – functions which are not mutually exclusive.

4 NVC may be correctly understood only in the total context of the situation. Signals such as those for intimacy can be understood only by attention to a combination of characteristics of behaviour.

5 We signal, receive and understand many forms of NVC without being consciously aware of it.

Chapter 13

Conformity

As chapters 5 and 6 have shown, the child learns to interact success-fully with its environment, including, very importantly, other people. He has to learn to take other people's feelings into account when planning his behaviour, to co-operate with others, and to behave in ways which they consider appropriate. Throughout life, the indivi-dual will meet many new people and will become a member of many different social groups. In the case of each group, different kinds of behaviour may be expected of him; he may have to *conform* to the behaviour of those around him.

What is Conformity?

Why do people conform? Do they have to be forced to do what other people want them to do, or do they do it willingly? It is tempting to equate conformity with uniformity or conventionality; but the definition of conformity by R.S. Crutchfield (1962) is 'yielding to group pressures'. This does not mean that a group actually forces the individual to behave in a particular way; the mere existence of a group belief may make some individuals conform to it, without overt force of any kind.

The study of the behaviour of the individual as a member of a group and the study of group behaviour generally is the province of a branch of psychology called 'social psychology' which studies how the individual's behaviour is affected by the group. The major experimenters in this area are M. Sherif, S. Asch, R.S. Crutchfield and S. Milgram who are all social psychologists. We shall look first at various demonstrations of conformity, and then at attempts to define levels of conformity and the situations in which it can be in-creased or decreased.

Muztafer Sherif (1935)

When a stationary spot of light is seen in a dark room it appears to move; this phenomenon is known as the *autokinetic effect*. Sherif used this effect, telling his subjects that he was going to move the light and asking them to report the extent of the movement. In a series of tests he found that each individual was very consistent in his estimates but that there were wide differences between the estimates of different subjects. However, when two or more subjects were tested together their estimates converged and became more similar (see table 24).

	Reported Movement when Tested:	
Subject	(a) Individually	(b) In the Group
A	4 in.	4.5 in.
B	1 in.	4 in.
C	7 in.	5 in.

Sherif had not told the subjects that they had to agree on the 'correct' figure, but each one could hear the others' estimates.

One defect of this experiment was that it provided no absolute correct answer against which the subjects' degrees of conformity could be measured. It would be better to conduct an experiment in which subjects had to answer questions for which there was a correct solution, so that their degrees of conformity relative to this could be gauged.

Solomon Asch (1951)

Asch realized this. Subjects were tested on simple perceptual tasks, such as deciding which of three lines was the same length as a standard line (see figure 44). Each subject was first tested separately. Only three mistakes were made when 36 subjects did about 20 trials each; therefore the task was an easy one. Subjects were then tested with a number of false subjects who were actually confederates of the experimenter. These people had been instructed to give incorrect answers on some of the trials. Under these conditions, if the stooge subjects said that line A in the figure was the same as the standard line, 32 per cent of the real subjects conformed and changed their

Figure 44. An Asch-type Figure

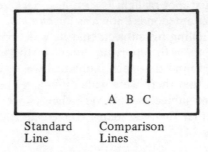

Standard   Comparison
Line   Lines

response from the correct answer, B, to A. 32 per cent conformed on all trials, but 74 per cent of subjects conformed at least some of the time.

The actual number of stooge subjects is important in such experiments. If there is only 1 real subject and 1 stooge, conformity is very low indeed: 'It's my word against yours.' The breaking point comes when there are 3 stooge subjects. Having more than 3 does not increase conformity much further. If, however, in a group of perhaps 13 stooges there are 2 real subjects the conformity level drops from 32 per cent to 6 per cent. The presence of another 'deviant' seems to help the subject to abide by his answer.

Richard Crutchfield (1954)

The type of experiment undertaken by Asch is very time-consuming as only one subject can be tested at a time. Crutchfield altered the experimental situation so that several subjects, usually 5, could be tested simultaneously. Each subject sat in a booth with an array of lights and switches in front of him. Subjects had to give answers to problems of the Asch type; each was told that he was the last to guess, and the guesses of the others were indicated by the lights on his panel. Of course each individual was actually given the same display, which was therefore incorrect on approximately half the trials.

Similar though generally lower conformity was found: 23 out of 50 – 46 per cent – of the military men tested agreed that the star in figure 45 had a larger area than the circle. Similar conformity was found when the subjects were tested on opinions. When tested privately, none of the 50 military men agreed with the statement 'I doubt whether I would make a good leader', but when given bogus agreements in their booths, 37 per cent did agree. Conformity

Figure 45. Type of Figure Used by Crutchfield

increases with the difficulty of the judgement being made; this finding matches Sherif's results. When the subjects were re-tested on the same items privately, most of their yielding disappeared.

Stanley Milgram (1963)

All the tests described so far indicate that real or even imagined group pressure can serve to make an individual conform to a group's decision. But all these conformities were only verbal and generally lasted only for the duration of the experiment. Milgram's work was different because his subjects had to show conformity – in the form of obedience to authority – in their actual behaviour. In order to conform fully they had to 'kill' another human being.

In his experiment which was conducted at Yale University, a real subject and a stooge subject drew lots to decide who would be teacher and learner in a 'memory experiment'. The stooge subject became the learner. The subject then watched while the stooge was strapped in a chair with his arms attached to electrodes which could give a shock. The subject was shown the shock generator and was given a mild shock himself to prove that it was real. The stooge subject warned the experimenter – who wore a lab-coat – that he had a heart condition, but he replied that the procedure could do 'little physical damage'. The subject then sat in a separate room with the shock generator, and asked the stooge simple memory questions. If the stooge responded wrongly – via a light system – the subject pressed a 15-volt button, and thereafter increased the shock by 15 volts each time an incorrect response was made. At about 150 volts the 'learner' started to complain; at about 250 volts he yelled 'Let me out! My heart's starting to bother me now!' at 300 volts he kicked the wall; and after this there was silence.

The experimenter supervised the arrangement, and followed a script of responses if the subject was unwilling to continue. The responses to the subject's protests increased in strength from: 'Please continue' or 'Please go on,' 'The experiment requires that you continue,' and 'It is absolutely essential that you continue,' to 'You have no other choice: you must go on.' In addition there were some 'special prods' which could be used to answer the subject's questions; for example, if the subject became worried about hurting the 'learner' the experimenter could say, 'Although the shocks may be painful, there is no permanent tissue damage, so please go on,' and if the subject felt that the 'learner' did not want to continue, 'Whether the learner likes it or not, you must go on until he has learnt all the word pairs correctly. So please go on.' Milgram described the experimental situation beforehand to psychiatrists, and asked them to predict how many people would give shocks as high as 450 volts. The reply was that less than 1 per cent would continue to this extreme level. However, in the actual experiment 62.5 per cent of the subjects went as far as 450 volts; all subjects who began giving shocks continued at least to 300 volts. These results were so much higher than common sense predicted that Milgram devised some alterations to the basic experiment to try to identify the factors which caused such high conformity.

First, many subjects reported that they had continued to 450 volts because the experiment was being carried out at Yale, an important American university. Milgram then ran the same experiments in a rather dilapidated office building away from the university so that subjects would not make any connection between the experiment and Yale University. The obedience level was still 50 per cent, a finding which suggests that although this reason was a factor in maintaining obedience it had probably not been a major one.

A second factor was the nearness of the 'learner'. Would the same levels of obedience be found if the 'learner' was in the same room as the subject, and could be seen by him? What would happen if the subject was required to hold the 'learner's' arm down on the electrodes? One might expect that the obedience level in the first case would be considerably lower than in the basic experiment and almost non-existent in the second case. In fact the obedience level when the 'learner' was in the same room as the subject and could be seen by him was 40 per cent. When the subject had to hold the 'learner's' arm down on the electrodes the obedience level was 30 per cent. In both cases there was therefore quite a large drop in the obedience level; nevertheless, it remained remarkably high considering the amount of information the subject was receiving about the effect of his reactions on the 'learner'. The nearness of the 'learner' was thus a factor but not as important a factor as one might expect.

Milgram believed that the major factor was therefore the presence of the experimenter in his lab coat. In situations where he left the room and issued instructions by telephone the obedience level dropped almost to zero: subjects would pretend to press the shock buttons, or press the button for a lesser shock than they ought to have given. Somehow the presence of the experimenter with his 'prods' compelled the subjects to carry on up to 450 volts.

According to Milgram, subjects must have been obeying the experimenter's position rather than his personality, which had been suppressed by his use of the script alone. To the subjects, the man in the lab coat appeared to know what was happening; many subjects kept turning to the experimenter for advice or reassurance. One important factor emerged: the experimenter was scripted to reply when asked if he would accept responsibility for what happened; once this had been established subjects complained very little and carried on with the experiment. Thus the experimenter's absence gave subjects a greater feeling of personal responsibility for their own actions, and prompted them to obey their own consciences rather than his instructions. For Milgram, then, the experimenter's position as an expert was the major factor in inducing obedience. Subjects knew little about what was happening, and therefore had to rely on the experimenter's word. When the experimenter accepted responsibility for what happened, this lifted the burden of uncertainty and fear that the subjects felt. Milgram draws parallels between the behaviour of his subjects and that of the Nazi war criminals in World War II. Often their plea was 'I was only obeying orders' – in other words, 'I did it, but somebody else higher up accepted responsibility for it.'

Perhaps it should be emphasized again that Milgram's experiment studied obedience to orders, unlike the other conformity experiments where subjects were not instructed to conform. The conformity of behaviour shown by Milgram's subjects was, however, much greater than that shown by subjects of Asch, Sherif and Crutchfield.

The conformity experiments have been criticized because they are set up in laboratories, and therefore not realistic. Critics make two main objections. First, subjects in conformity experiments are not allowed to discuss the problem with others or to get more information. Crutchfield counters this by saying that in real life, too, discussion is limited, and that all the facts are not known; in some situations there are no facts or correct answers at all, only opinions. The fact that a group believes something may actually prevent its members from looking for further evidence about it. The second objection is that conformity experiments often involve deception on the part of the experimenter, particularly those of Asch and Milgram. It is undoubtedly morally wrong to deceive subjects, especially if an experiment is upsetting to them. But at the same time real life itself involves deception – through propaganda, advertising and the biased arguments of politics, for example.

Types of Conformity – Compliance and Internalization

H. Kelman (1958) proposes that there are really two types of conformity – *compliance*, when the subject outwardly agrees with the group to save argument but inwardly disagrees, and *internalization*, when the subject conforms because he believes or trusts the answers given by the rest of the group.

Sherif's experiment with the autokinetic phenomenon seems to be a clear case of internalization. Because there is no right answer, subjects' replies converge; they may be unaware that this is happening and believe that their own answers are correct. They will not be aware that they have deviated from their individual pattern of response towards that of the other subjects.

Asch's study showed mainly the compliance type of conformity. Nearly all the subjects reverted to their original answers when removed from the group's pressure. However, Asch performed an experiment similar to that involving line judgement in which he asked his subjects to state their strength of agreement or disagreement with statements such as 'I feel that the unions are allowed too much power in this country.' He found that most subjects conformed just as they had in the perceptual tasks, but in this case some subjects showed internalization: when asked, individually, the same question two weeks later, 50 per cent of the subjects gave the same answer as the group had given. The reason that many subjects internalized in the second Asch experiment was that there was no obviously right answer to the problem as there was with the perceptual task.

Did the subjects in Milgram's experiment show compliance or internalization? It is difficult to say. Most felt severe guilt at what they had done, and outside the laboratory afterwards were shocked at their behaviour. But would they be more willing or less willing to obey similar commands in future? Either event could occur: a subject might either be sickened by what had happened and refuse to obey similar commands, thus demonstrating compliance, or take refuge in the 'my leader, right or wrong' attitude which implies identification with the experimenter.

The conformity and obedience experiments stress the important influence that others have on an individual's behaviour. Much of the behaviour and many of the opinions of a person are the result of these outside forces. This means that there is a much greater uniformity within groups of people than we might expect if we considered them as single individuals.

Summary

1 Conformity can be defined as 'yielding to group pressures'.
2 Sherif's experiment with the autokinetic phenomenon showed how conformity can occur in a group, even when none of the group has been told that they have to agree.
3 Asch's experiment showed that individuals will conform to the behaviour of a group of stooge subjects even when the group's response is obviously wrong. The minimum number of stooge subjects required seems to be three; the presence of two real subjects reduces conformity considerably.
4 Crutchfield's experiments modified Asch's so that more subjects could be dealt with in a shorter time. They demonstrated a slightly lower degree of conformity, which increased with the difficulty of the task.
5 Milgram's experiment was really testing obedience to authority; subjects were given orders which they were told to follow. They showed obedience by giving electric shocks to another, stooge, subject. Milgram believed that the cause of the high obedience rate was mainly subjects' deference to the experimenter's role as an expert in that situation; when he accepted responsibility for whatever might happen, subjects were more likely to continue.
6 Kelman proposed that there were two major types of conformity, compliance – paying lip service – and internalization – believing. If an individual adopts a group's attitude after the experiment it is internalization; if he returns to his former attitude it is compliance.

Chapter 14

Work

If we accept the ideas of Piaget, Bruner and Heim the purpose of development is to enable the individual to cope with his environment. In this chapter we shall be concerned with a kind of environment which plays a very large part in most people's adult lives – the working environment. Obviously the physical aspects of the environment can have an effect on the individual; for example, people can die of exposure to the cold, and there are physical factors, other than temperature, which also influence our behaviour. Although it is generally accepted that people work best in a 'good' physical environment it is hard to define what a 'good' environment means.

It would, for example, be quite easy to set up an experiment in a factory in order to investigate the effects of temperature on the individual's ability to work. We could measure how much an individual produced in a given time at 30°C, 15°C and 0°C, and it is likely that his output would be highest at 15°C: as one would expect, extreme environmental conditions can have adverse effects upon performance. However, we might also find quite large differences in the ability of individuals to cope with such changing conditions; we might even find that some subjects performed better at the higher or the lower temperature. Thus it is possible to specify what constitutes a good working environment in general terms, but it must always be remembered that different individuals can react differently to the same environment; what is 'good' for one individual may be 'bad' for another.

In the first part of this section, therefore, in which we examine the effects of various physical environmental variables on behaviour at work, please bear this point in mind.

The Effects of Environmental Variables on Behaviour

Although findings in this area are probably not applicable to every individual, it nevertheless seems possible to formulate an overall law which describes the effects of physical variables on working perform-ance. This is known as the *Yerkes–Dodson Law*. It states that the level of arousal – explained below – affects the level of an individual's performance in the following way: in general, a low level of arousal leads to low performance; a moderate level of arousal leads to high performance; and a high level of arousal leads to low performance. This is perhaps better explained in the graph form of figure 46.

Figure 46. The Yerkes–Dodson Law

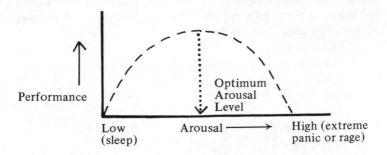

Arousal can be defined as the level of excitation of an organism: low arousal would mean that an individual was sleepy; moderate arousal would mean that he was awake and alert; and high arousal would mean that he was in a state of over-excitement or high tension. You will remember from page 87 that biofeedback machines, using gal-vanic skin response, can be employed to measure in a rough way the level of arousal. You can see from figure 46, then, that there is a point of arousal – marked 'optimum' – which results in the highest or optimum level of performance. If the performance be-ing measured is the driving of a car, at a low level of arousal the individual concerned will be likely to make mistakes because he will not react quickly enough, will make miscalculations and will be generally slow-witted. As his arousal increases his performance will improve. There will come a point at which he will be driving at peak efficiency and effectiveness. However, if his arousal continues to increase beyond this optimum point his performance level will begin to fall again. He will tend to make hasty, ill-controlled movements and will again be liable to miscalculations; the highest level of arousal may even manifest itself as paralysis with fear or speechless rage. Whether arousal is caused by fear or rage the effect will be the same: he will drive badly, if at all.

The optimum level of arousal for a simple task is generally higher than that for a complex one: performance on a simple task is less affected by an increase in arousal than performance on a complex task. Thus if two people, A and B, worked in the same environment, with A doing a complex task and B a simple one, and they were subjected to some kind of environmental stress, such as an increase in the temperature or the amount of noise, we should expect A's performance to suffer first, because an increase in arousal usually harms performance on a complex task more readily. Bearing in mind the Yerkes–Dodson Law, we shall now examine how environmental variables can affect behaviour.

Figure 47. The Interaction Between Complexity of Task and Level of Arousal

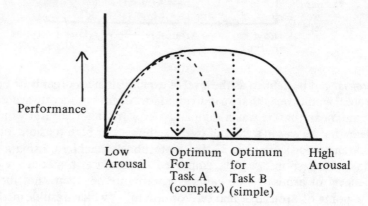

Temperature

As the temperature rises the body has more difficulty in disposing of unwanted body heat; in addition to temperature, humidity – the level of moisture in the atmosphere – plays an important part. On a hot, dry day the body sweats but because the air is dry the sweat can evaporate easily and cool the body down; on an equally hot, humid day, however, the sweat cannot evaporate so easily and one feels hotter. Also the more physical effort involved in an activity, the more heat the body will produce. Thus the worst possible work environment in terms of temperature would be one in which the temperature was hot, the humidity was high and the worker was doing heavy, physical labour.

Research findings suggest that when the skin temperature rises to 45°C the individual experiences very severe pain and that prolonged exposure to such an environment can cause tissue damage, to both the skin and lungs. Below this level there are fairly wide individual differences in heat tolerance, which seem to depend at least partly on age (the older, the less heat tolerance); physical fitness (the less fit, the less heat tolerance); and length of acclimatization (the shorter the period of acclimatization, the less heat tolerance). If an individual is suddenly subjected to an increase in temperature this seems to increase his arousal level at first, but as his body temperature begins to rise his arousal level falls. Thus people often become sleepy when they enter a warm room and stay in it for any length of time. According to the Yerkes–Dodson graph, then, increasing temperature will have the effect of reducing arousal level and therefore of reducing performance.

Noise

Noise, or unwanted sound, is usually measured in decibels, which is a scale of the amplitude (see page 37) produced by a sound stimulus. One of the lowest levels of noise – 10 decibels – would be like the rustle of leaves in a gentle breeze; the noises in an average home would read 40 on the decibel scale; a busy street would register 70 decibels; a tube-train heard from the distance of six metres would record 95 decibels; the loudest clap of thunder would be measured at 120 decibels; and the noise six metres away from a jet engine with an after-burner would give a decibel reading of 140. Research findings suggest that noise levels of 90 decibels and above can cause decreases in performance. Fairly prolonged exposure of half an hour or more to such noise levels results in momentary lapses of attention which in turn reduce performance. However, lower levels of noise which are not continuous but which appear and disappear suddenly may also influence performance, though their effects seem to depend on what kind of task is being performed. Thus occasional bursts of noise of 80 decibels seem to improve performance on boring, repetitive tasks – presumably because the sudden stimulus they provide increases arousal; on more complex tasks, however, similar bursts of 80-decibel noise, as one might expect from the Yerkes–Dodson curve, seem to reduce performance level because they increase arousal beyond the optimum point.

It is not only the level of noise which is important but also its frequency. This is why a fairly quiet noise like chalk squeaking on a blackboard is hardly noticed by some people but can make others squirm in discomfort.

In addition the effects of noise on the performance of a laboratory task, for example, may be different from those on the performance of the same task in a factory environment: if a certain job requires communication and a worker has to shout to his neighbour or to repeat sentences in order to be heard because of the noise, he is liable to become annoyed, his arousal level will rise and his performance will suffer.

Lighting

You will remember from chapter 2 that rods and cones have different functions, and that the edges of the retinas contain far more rods than cones while the fovea, the area of clearest vision, is made totally of cones. If we regard the fovea as having 100 per cent accuracy of vision, then the retinal cells only 10° away from it must have only about 40 per cent accuracy and cells 40° away 20 per cent accuracy. In a work situation this fact would necessitate maximum illumination roughly within the central 30° of the individual's field of vision.

The type of task involved will, however, affect the optimum illumination level required: for a task which entails close visual inspection of something the fovea will be the most important part of the retina and consequently its cones will require a fairly high illumination level; but for tasks which do not require detailed inspection – for example, tasks in which the worker is required to use his peripheral vision in scanning a range of simple dials – no particular importance need be given to the illumination of the central 30° of the visual field. You will remember also that foveal vision registers colour while peripheral vision detects very little, if any. It would therefore make sense in designing a working environment for a job which involves distinguishing between lights of different colours to concentrate any stimuli which involve colour in the central 30° of the visual field, because colours outside this area will be far less likely to be correctly recognized. We can therefore say that, the more visually detailed the task, the greater the illumination level required. Thus the level of illumination over an operating table would need to be very high; general office work would not require anywhere near as high a level of illumination; and loading and unloading lorries would need even less light.

Another factor which can affect the importance of illumination is the amount of light reflected by objects upon which the illumination falls. Because paper reflects more light than coal, the illumination level required to see the paper is much lower than that required to see coal. The percentage of light which an object reflects is called its *albedo*; white paper reflects about 90 per cent of the light which hits it, so its albedo level is 90 per cent, while coal has a low albedo level of about 10 per cent. If the optimum level of illumination for inspecting coal were to be arranged for paper inspection we should probably find that the inspectors would very soon suffer from glare. The optimum illumination level should therefore always be designed to take the albedo factor into account, as well as the complexity of the visual task. As with temperature, extremes of illumination level will have adverse effects on performance, even though illumination may not actually affect arousal. One could substitute level of illumination for arousal on the Yerkes–Dodson graph and probably still achieve the same curve.

Stress
As we have seen, the Yerkes–Dodson Law indicates that arousal affects performance. *Stress* might be defined as any variable which increases arousal, particularly if it causes it to exceed the optimum level. Noise, illumination and temperature in excess may all lead to too great an increase in arousal or stress, but stress can also occur in other ways. Knowledge of failure can be a factor; while this can sometimes cause a low arousal level to reach the optimum level, it may also increase it too far. An individual may then appear to be 'trying too hard'. In addition people who have to do several things at once or to deal with a large amount of sensory information quickly can become stressed – partly because they are making more mistakes which they will have to put right, thus further overloading themselves, and partly because they are aware that they are not coping successfully.

Circadian/Diurnal Rhythms

If you had to work for a full twenty-four hours, how would your performance be affected? If you started work at 9 a.m. and finished the following day at 9 a.m. you might expect your performance to decline as time went on. Of course a good deal of this decline would be caused by the build-up of fatigue because you would be losing sleep, but sleep research suggests that some other factor is involved in the decline as well.

If we remove the effects of fatigue, simply by measuring performance for short periods of time so that the subject may be doing only three hours work per day but at different times each day, we find

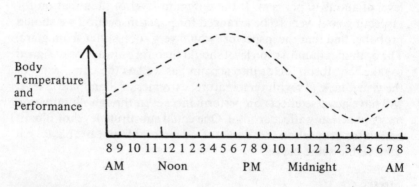

Figure 48. *The Variation of Body Temperature and Performance Over a 24-hour Period*

that performance is lower at some times than at others. Nathaniel Kleitman, a sleep-research psychologist, suggested that speed of reaction – as a measure of performance – varies over the twenty-four-hour period, with a peak level of performance in mid-afternoon, and a low point at about 4 to 5 a.m. Along with this variation in performance, Kleitman found that body temperature showed a corresponding variation; in fact the correlation between body temperature and performance was $+0.89$. It must be remembered, however, that correlation does not imply causation; the fact that the two measures' variations corresponded does not necessarily mean that one characteristic causes the other, in fact it is not true that low body temperature causes low performance in this case. We could show this by artificially increasing body temperature. If this directly influenced performance, raising body temperature should increase performance. However, this is not the result. It must be that some other factor can cause both body temperature and performance to drop.

Work by M. Jouvet, a French psychologist, suggests that sleep occurs when the reticular activating system (see page 18) is inhibited by serotonin and noradrenalin which are secreted by structures near it. This activity may be the mysterious 'other factor', but we do not yet know why this inhibition of the RAS occurs. As a hypothesis only, it may be that humans have evolved to live in a twenty-four-hour day and that there is some biological need for sleep which has evolved in this twenty-four-hour cycle. Some internal 'body clock' may prompt the inhibition of the RAS on a regular basis.

Whatever the cause of this *circadian rhythm*, it does seem to affect performance as Kleitman noted. It also seems to be flexible: individuals can adapt to a different twenty-four-hour cycle from their normal one, as airline passengers suffering from jet lag, and night-shift workers, eventually do. Thus in studies of jet lag air travellers who cross international time-lines find their 'body' time out of phase with the time of the country in which they arrive. Studies of airline pilots show that when they fly from the USA to Germany they gain 8 hours (that is, if they leave the USA at 1 p.m. USA time, even though the flight may take 4 hours, which would make their arrival time 5 p.m. in USA time, the actual time in Germany is 1 a.m.). So they are out of phase with everybody in Germany; in effect, they are 8 hours behind everybody there. It takes them several days, perhaps a week, to adjust their 'body clocks' to European time; thus the confusion of somebody who constantly travels across time zones can be easily imagined. His 'peak' and 'low' performance periods will be out of phase with his new environment and he may take a week to adapt, by which time he has crossed yet another time zone, and the process of adaptation must begin all over again.

Night-shift workers, provided that they are on permanent night shift, can adapt to this arrangement, and their body rhythms can be displaced by twelve hours, so that their peak performance can occur around 4–5 a.m. – when most day workers have their 'low'. However, the alternation between day and night shifts does not allow this to happen, with consequent reduction in performance. (Incidentally, home conditions, particularly the amount of sound-proofing in the bedroom, can affect a night-shift worker's performance quite markedly.)

Why Do People Work?

Physical environment can affect performance, but it is only one influence. Most people would not rate 'physical environment' highest if they were choosing a job, because physical environment does not influence our psychological motivation as much as other factors. The following summary of the Hawthorne experiment shows that, while the physical environment can affect performance, other, psychological factors may have a still greater effect.

An experiment was carried out to investigate the effects on performance of different lighting levels. Each environmental variable was altered in turn; the workers were interviewed after each change to find out how they felt about it; and their output was then measured. Increasing the illumination level increased production; so did giving longer and more frequent rest pauses, providing shorter working hours, and so on. Then the investigators decided to decrease the light level, even to the dimness of moonlight. Production still increased. The investigators then removed all the improvements which had been introduced so that working conditions reverted to the standards which had existed before the investigation began. However, production still increased. What was causing this increase? The investigators, F.J. Roethlisberger and W.J. Dickson (1939), at the Hawthorne plant of the General Electric Co. in Chicago, decided that what had caused the general increase in production was the fact that they had interviewed the workers concerned. It seems that workers had felt themselves to be 'special' because their views were being asked for; they were receiving more attention and interest. When a large-scale interview programme was extended to the whole factory, production in its other sections also increased.

Behaviourists would term this effect *social reinforcement*; it contradicts another theory that the major reason why people work harder is to get money. This belief, tested experimentally by F.W. Taylor, seemed to suggest that the use of increased wages would enable managers to persuade their workforces to work harder and more efficiently. However, Taylor deliberately chose workers who demonstrated their love of money. While for them, perhaps, Taylor's theory holds true, we cannot apply these findings to all workers. Later research suggests that while money can be an important motivator it is by no means always so: security, enjoyable work and even the chance to join a union can be more important than money in motivating a workforce.

The value of money as a motivator is difficult to assess, however. Behaviourists would say that if an increase in production is desired, any upward trend in production should be immediately reinforced. In most factories immediate – even day-to-day – reinforcement is not possible; some research suggests that increases in earnings are more likely to be given on the basis of appearance and punctuality, rather than efficiency. Until it has been shown that reinforcing increased efficiency with money does not work, it must be assumed to play at least some part in motivation. The problem in identifying money, or working conditions, as the most important motivator is that theories are often derived from studies of individuals, and the behaviour of an individual working on his own can be different from his behaviour when working in a group. Offering increased wages for increased production may be effective up to a point, but at the same time groups of workers develop a group attitude to their rate of working: individuals who try to exceed this rate or do not work hard enough are often pressured by the group to conform to its pace. (You will also remember from the earlier studies on conformity and obedience that individuals may conform to a group's behaviour, even when no overt pressure is put on them.)

The studies at the Hawthorne plant, then, showed that social factors could be important as motivators and that money was certainly not the only possible motivator. So far we have identified two types of motivator – money, and interest from superiors. Is it possible to identify other kinds? Abraham Maslow produced a theory of motivation which sought to include all possible motivators. He produced a list of five needs arranged in a hierarchy, and argued that a more basic or low-level need must be satisfied before a higher need becomes important (see table on page 194). Thus safety needs will only become important as motivators when physiological needs have been satisfied, social needs will become important when safety needs are satisfied, and so on. However, Maslow points out that while this need hierarchy can be applied to humans generally, an individual may change levels daily; for example, one day an individual may be motivated by social needs primarily, but as he gets hungry, physiological needs will become predominant. In addition some individuals may not reach the higher levels. The need for self-actualization is regarded by Maslow as the most developed level; in other

194   BEGINNING PSYCHOLOGY

Higher Needs	5	Self-actualization — need for self-development, for realizing one's potential
	4	Self-respect and esteem — need for self- confidence, knowledge, competence, status, respect
	3	Social needs — need for acceptance by peers, friendship, etc.
Basic Needs	2	Safety needs — protection against danger, need for security
	1	Physiological needs — for survival, food, water, shelter

words, humans sometimes engage in some forms of behaviour simply because they enjoy it.

While Maslow's hierarchy is a useful way of describing the various types of motivators, there are great difficulties in predicting what will motivate an individual at any particular time. Five individuals at work may each be at any of the five different levels, and there is no suggestion in the theory about how demanding each of the needs is (what, for example, an individual requires to satisfy his safety need); different individuals may have different amounts of the same need, and therefore require differing amounts of satisfaction. Nevertheless, Maslow's hierarchy reminds us that motivators can differ not only between individuals but also within an individual at different times. It indicates the complexities of the question, what motivates people to work?

D. McGregor calls Taylor's view of motivation – that people work because they are rewarded for doing so or in order to avoid punishment – theory X. Following on from this, people must be strictly controlled at work, and will prefer this anyway, because they will not desire any responsibility. In opposition to this he puts forward theory Y, proposing that people have a natural desire to work, can show self-discipline, seek responsibility and are creative, but are prevented from making use of these attributes by modern industrial organization. Theory Y suggests that if the aims of individual and organization can be linked then these human qualities can be harnessed to further the aims of industrial organization.

F. Herzberg proposed that two major categories of factors

affected the job satisfaction and motivation of workers. He asked individuals to report instances where they had felt satisfaction about their jobs and instances where they had felt dissatisfaction. Statistical analysis of these results indicated that one category of factors, *motivators*, created job satisfaction, while the other, *hygiene factors*, created dissatisfaction with such things as company policy, supervision and working conditions. Thus motivators are concerned with the job itself and how well the individual performs it, while hygiene factors are concerned with the organization and the working environment. Herzberg's belief was that if the motivators are provided job satisfaction follows, but that although 'good' hygiene factors prevent job dissatisfaction they do not necessarily lead to job satisfaction.

Problems have arisen with this theory because when during the studies individuals were asked to talk or write about their job satisfaction, other individuals acting as judges analysed their statements and tried to identify which factors caused satisfaction or dissatisfaction. Thus there was a risk of bias in the results: the judges may have found what they wanted to find rather than what was actually there. In addition it may be that individuals believe that satisfaction is caused by their own efforts but dissatisfaction is caused by the management, the working environment and other people, and is not their own fault. This may have led to a biased summary of hygiene and motivator factors. Herzberg's theory is no longer held in such high regard because later evidence does not support it; but as one of the first investigations of job satisfaction it has proved valuable in indicating the potential importance of self-motivation, a view which is equally recognized by Maslow.

E.H. Schein summarizes the various theories by devising four types of individual:

1 Rational–economic (Taylor man).

2 Social (Hawthorne man).

3 Self-actualizing (Maslow and Herzberg man).

4 Complex – an individual who can at different times and in different environments demonstrate any or all of these kinds of motivation. Thus within a firm individuals at different levels of responsibility may be motivated by different factors – salesmen perhaps by social needs; workers on repetitive, boring, noisy jobs by money; research workers by self-actualization or curiosity, and so on.

The available research does not provide any solution to industrial problems but it warns us against magic recipes for industrial and commercial success and contentment. Because we have identified the possible motivators we can at least use this 'check-list' to improve motivation and promote job satisfaction to some extent. As a result of Hawthorne, Maslow and McGregor's work, job-enrichment procedures have been created which involve encouraging an individual to play a larger role at work – to take on more responsibilities, increase his range of skills, and perform more aspects of an activity instead of being limited to a single task.

Working and Groups

The Hawthorne studies illustrated how the existence of groups could be important at work. In some of their later researches Roethlisberger and Dickson found that individuals who worked as part of a group but broke the group's 'rules' were often made to conform again by gentle persuasion, argument, 'sending to Coventry', or occasionally even by violence. 'Rate busters', individuals who worked at a faster rate than that tacitly established by the group, could in these ways be persuaded to perform at the group's rate. Conversely it can happen that a job which in most respects may be unpleasant can become quite bearable if the working group of which the individual is a member 'get along together'; even then, however, the group can control his behaviour to some extent. Thus a group can both positively reinforce behaviour which is acceptable and negatively reinforce it by ceasing group pressure only when unacceptable behaviour is dropped.

A group's behaviour may be different from the behaviour of any of its individuals acting independently. However, it is a mistake to think of the group as a 'super-individual'. Statements such as 'The group thinks. . . .' or 'The group wants. . . .' do not really make sense. There is no being called a 'group'; instead its activities, beliefs and needs are the result of a multitude of interactions between its individuals. Throughout life, humans are members of groups. In infancy and childhood through to adolescence we are members of family groups, but we also gradually form friendship groups outside the family. It is therefore a logical development that we should also form groups at work; indeed groups for some types of work – for example ship's crews, miners, bricklaying gangs and production teams in industry – are essential.

From the individual's point of view why is it in his interests to join a working group? What is the reinforcement for doing so? According to G. Homans (1951), there are two major factors involved. First, because of the way in which modern industry is organized, when an individual gets a job this can often only be carried out as a member of a team or group. As humans have developed more numerous and specialized skills it has become difficult for any single individual to master all those involved in a particular industry. Consequently firms have developed a system of division of labour whereby an individual may be required to learn only one type of skill and to perform this over and over again. Each process in a manufacturing industry is then carried out by a separate group which specializes in one kind of activity. Groups of workers who practise the same skills will therefore be kept together, performing their specialized task in a particular area of the factory.

The second type of factor, social approval in the form of praise and attention and interaction with other people, can be a reinforcer, as we discussed in chapter 9 on imitation and identification and chapter 5 on learning. Groups can provide much reinforcement in a variety of forms, as suggested by Maslow's hierarchy of needs: safety, social and self-respect needs can be satisfied by groups. A group can thus both help to get a job more efficiently done by division of labour and provide social reinforcement for its individuals by satisfying social needs in the same way as family and friendship groups do for most people.

In theory a working group's job is to work: the social functions of the group are supposed to be of secondary importance to its work function. In practice the two functions may sometimes be compatible with one another, while at other times they may create conflicts of priorities for the individual and the group. The extent to which a group can achieve success in its primary task – work – and its secondary task – social relationships – often depends on how strongly the group is bound together, or its *cohesiveness*. A highly cohesive group can fulfil work requirements well, especially when a task necessitates co-operation among its members; the group can also provide more opportunities for social reinforcement. A less cohesive group will co-operate less well, and there will probably be much less social reinforcement given the individual by others in the group. Several factors play a part in determining the cohesiveness of a group – group size, work locations, the similarity of the work done, work flow, and status or prestige.

First, roughly eight to ten people can communicate with each other face to face. Above this number face-to-face contact becomes more difficult, and there is the possibility with too large a group that it will split into two or more face-to-face groups. Secondly, individuals who work close together are more likely to form cohesive groups: a group with its members scattered in the four corners of a factory will have great difficulty in internal communications. Also, doing the same job as others provides some basis for interaction; the same jobs are often kept in the same area of a factory. The system of work flow, too, can have an effect. If members of a group are strung out along a production line stretching over a hundred yards they will have great difficulty in communicating with each other. Finally, the status and prestige factor is important because a group which is respected for its efficiency or liked greatly by others will become more cohesive.

The fact that a group is cohesive, however, is not always an advantage; a highly cohesive group can seriously hinder the likelihood of success in certain cases. The effect of cohesiveness depends on the group's attitude to its work and to the organization which employs it. Let us take two extremes, both highly cohesive groups, one of which, A, is very much in favour of the management of its firm, and the other, B, which is against the management. Group A sees its aims as identical to those of the management; we might expect statements from its members such as, 'We're all pulling together in this firm' or, 'Leave the job to us; we'll get it done.' This group will work hard and be flexible in overcoming obstacles. It will see its main aim as getting the job done, and to this end its members will help and support each other. On the other hand group B is against the management in whatever it does. Any changes are viewed as threats or attempts to get more work for less pay. The individuals are highly cohesive but their aim might be expressed as, 'We're not going to let them get the better of us!' Their cohesion will help to prevent the job being completed by slow working, downing tools at the slightest provocation, refusal to try anything different, and so on.

The individuals who constitute a group gradually develop shared ideas and beliefs about what the group should be doing. These ideas and beliefs, which influence the individual's behaviour, are termed *norms*; for example, a working group may develop a low-output norm. Any individual who works counter to this will be pressured to conform, and if he does not he may be expelled from the group, or will at least lose much social reinforcement. Thus, within the formal organization of a firm, an informal organization of groups can develop, whose aims may be the opposite of those of the larger body. A group may not even know what the general aims of its firm are; its members may never have been told, or alternatively the group may be well informed but feel that the company's aims have been dictated by others, are not relevant to them and are beyond their control (sometimes expressed in the attitude of some supervisors as 'You're not paid to think – work.')

Even when the aims of firm and group do not conflict, a firm may be unaware of a group's social needs, requiring high output but not realizing that the working environment may, for example, make communication more difficult for group members. In this case the group may begin to work more slowly by taking rest breaks more frequently and by spending more time talking on the job; it may start to develop low-output norms if no improvement in conditions is made.

Particularly in small groups each individual plays a part in forming group decisions. However, the more members there are in an informal group, the greater the chance that a group leader will emerge. Such leaders are often termed informal leaders because they have no official position; nevertheless, they can often profoundly influence the development of group norms.

Group Leaders

The informal group leader's power is usually gained through his own skills in persuasion, because he has no official power over the group. An informal group may have more than one informal leader; for example, it may have one leader for job activities, who is selected by the group for his particular job skills, and a second, 'opinion', leader, again chosen by the group because of his persuasive powers or because he will stand up to the management. The formal leader or supervisor may have official power to control the group, but his effectiveness can be outweighed by the influence of the group's informal leaders. Some management theorists now advise that managers should consult particularly with the informal leaders in an organization: if they can be persuaded to accept a new scheme they are more likely to persuade their informal groups to do so. The suggestion is also made that such leaders and their groups should be involved in making the decisions in the first place, in the belief that if an informal group helps to make a decision it is more likely to implement it than if the decision is simply dictated from outside.

The leader of an informal group is often chosen by its members for some personal quality – usually for how likeable he is, if he is to be the 'social' leader of the group, for example. Some 'work' leaders of informal groups, on the other hand, may even be chosen because they are awkward and argumentative: individuals in the group may feel that they need somebody capable of confronting the management. Most informal group leaders are chosen or emerge as a result of the free choice and common agreement of all the members of the group; the process is a democratic one. On the other hand the formal leader may be imposed on the group by the management, and will therefore not be democratically chosen within the group itself. He may not even be liked by any members of the group. Although he is supposed to look after both its work and social needs he is often in practice chosen only for his working skills or knowledge of the job.

As we saw earlier, the working and social aims of the group can affect each other; a group leader who ignores one or the other has little chance of being supported. A formal leader may excel at a particular job but if his social relationship with the group is poor, he may find that its members work against him, so that even with his special knowledge the job is performed poorly. The way in which a leader leads his group can thus have important effects on individuals' attitudes to their jobs and how successfully they work.

The classic study of the effects of different styles of leadership was performed by Lewin, Lippitt and White in 1938 (see page 157). Later studies in industry support these findings. In one such study a factory which had been run on traditional autocratic lines was taken over by another firm and workers were encouraged to take part in decision making. After two years of the democratic style of leadership the absentee rate had been cut by half and the amount of goods produced per week had risen by a third. The democratic style of leadership has much to recommend it, but there are also problems and dangers: if all members of a group are encouraged to help make decisions, decisions may take a long time. This is obviously a drawback in situations where quick decisions are essential, so that a compromise in style of leadership may be the most practicable solution:

a group can be allowed to make its own decisions except in cases of urgency, when the leader or group expert alone will resolve the issue.

Because there is such a wide variety of work, groups, leaders, and organizational and individual needs, a single leadership style is unlikely to become a cure-all for industrial and commercial problems. A greater understanding of how and why groups affect the individual would be beneficial, because it would lead to a greater flexibility of approach to industrial problems.

Summary

1 The physical environment influences the individual's performance. Most humans work efficiently only within a relatively narrow range within each of the environmental variables – heat, light, noise and stress for example. The Yerkes–Dodson Law enables us to predict the effects of these variables.

2 The circadian rhythm or internal 'body clock' of the individual also affects his performance. Shift work and jet lag can induce alterations to this rhythm.

3 Early theories about why people work concentrated on the need for money. The studies at the Hawthorne plant showed that social factors at work could be more important.

4 Maslow argued that each individual has a hierarchy of five needs; the lowest of these must be satisfied before the next need in the hierarchy is felt. The needs of different individuals may vary in similar situations, both in nature and intensity; in addition an individual may experience different kinds of needs during one day.

5 Herzberg proposed that the factors leading to job satisfaction – motivators – were positive reinforcers while those leading to dissatisfaction – hygiene factors – were negative reinforcers.

6 Schein believed that no one theory could account for all work motivation. An individual can be motivated by different things at different times, depending on the level of his job, the amount of stimulation he receives, his chances of success, money and so on.

7 Groups at work influence the individual's attitudes and motivation. The group may be an informal one which is not part of the official hierarchy of the firm; its aims may conflict with those of the company as a whole. If the aims of the firm and the group can be

made identical, however, informal groups may help a firm to operate more efficiently.

8 Within a group a leader often emerges; sometimes a group may have different leaders for each of its different activities. Style of leadership can affect the success of the group's effort: a style which is generally democratic seems to encourage better results than authoritarian or *laissez-faire* styles.

Chapter 15

Ageing

Much of the work of psychologists is concerned with the early years of the individual's development. This is understandable: the individual's development during the first few years of life may have quite profound effects on later behaviour. But development does not stop at adulthood; if 'development' means change, then we develop throughout life. We shall now consider whether this later development helps the individual to adapt better to his environment or whether it is simply a process of deterioration.

There are two traditional attitudes to the course of development as we age:

1 'The older, the wiser.' As we get older we store more information, learn more skills and can do more.

2 'You can't teach an old dog new tricks.' As we get older we become fixed in our ways and resistant to change; we deteriorate physically and mentally.

Which of these apparently opposite adages is true? What happens to the individual physically, mentally and socially as he ages?

'You Can't Teach An Old Dog New Tricks'

Some of the changes which accompany ageing are easy to see. The skin becomes less supple; it becomes wrinkled and loses its youthful bloom; teeth may fall out and gums recede; loss of hair is common in males; heart output declines, and so on. However, other changes occur which are not so easily visible and are only detected when appropriate tests have been made. Some of these indicate that increasing age does lead to a deterioration in performance. We shall now look at the findings.

Short-Term Memory or STM

If a list of seven digits or letters is read out at the rate of one per second, and subjects are asked to recall them immediately, older people recall slightly fewer correctly. If we repeat this type of test, then ask the subjects to do some unrelated task – for example, recite the alphabet backwards – and then after a few seconds ask them to recall the list, older people will perform markedly worse than younger people.

Short-term memory is therefore a process by which information can be stored very quickly in the brain and recalled within a few seconds. After this brief period, if the information is not recalled or rehearsed it will be forgotten. Consider someone looking up a telephone number in the telephone directory. He looks up the number and can then remember it long enough to dial it, but a few seconds after he has done this, if asked to recall it, he will probably be unable to do so. If he is in any way distracted, by the time he is ready to dial the number it will have gone from his short-term memory and he will have to look it up again.

Thus distraction tasks in experiments, like reciting the alphabet backwards for a few seconds, interfere with STM. Older people seem to be much more vulnerable to this interference than young people, and, as we shall see later, their vulnerability can have quite marked effects on their performance of a job.

Reaction Time

In a typical reaction-time experiment the subject is given a stimulus such as a light going on or a buzzer sounding, and has to press a button as quickly as possible in response to it. The time which elapses between the appearance of the stimulus and the subject's finger hitting the button is the *reaction time*. In this kind of test, older people are only slightly slower than younger people. However, if the complexity of the task is increased – for example by using a red and a green light and two buttons, so that the subject has to press a button only when the light above it is on – older subjects do much worse than younger subjects.

It used to be thought that they performed such tasks more slowly because their muscles worked more slowly or because their vision or hearing was defective, but it is now thought that the major cause is an increase in *decision time*. This is the time taken for the brain to recognize that there is a stimulus present, select the response to set in operation and order the muscles to move appropriately; thus the more complex the decision which has to be made, the longer the decision time. This is true for people of all ages, but for older people the decision time is much longer than for young people.

A.T. Welford proposes that the decline with age of the two processes, short-term memory and speed of decision making, has a great influence on the performance of older people at work. He suggests that an older worker can still perform satisfactorily but that he will be working nearer to the limits of his abilities than he did when younger. While his speed and strength of movement may not have declined much, his general performance will nevertheless be hampered by his weakest abilities; consequently as he gets older his STM and speed of reaction will limit his performance.

Consider the case of an older worker performing a skilled job which requires accurate perception of what is happening to the objects he is manipulating. Any reduction in his muscular strength will be unlikely to affect his performance much, for he is probably working well within his muscular capacity. If, however, the skilled job involves the need to make frequent and quick decisions we should expect a decline in performance: his decision-making time will be relatively long and he will be working at near or full capacity. Any sudden extra decisions will overload him; he will have too much to do at once, and so his performance will suffer. R.L. Gregory, among others, has proposed that this may be due to the older person's brain working less efficiently. All neurons, in addition to firing when they are stimulated by others, sometimes fire spontaneously, without any external stimulation. Normally this random firing is not noticed by the individual, but it is thought that ageing increases the amount of random firing in the brain. Consequently, just as you would have difficulty in hearing a telephone conversation when there was a lot of interference on the line, so the brain activity which is involved in decision making may be masked by the interference due to the random firing of neurons elsewhere in the brain. Since the decision-making signals in the brain are not as clear as they once were, the individual may take longer to verify a decision, so that the time needed for him to reach a decision increases.

The performance of the older worker will suffer if a job makes demands on his short-term memory – particularly if it involves his memorizing something, holding it in STM while he does something else, and then recalling it. Alternatively his performance will deteriorate if he has to remember elaborate instructions, overloading his STM, or work fast, overloading his decision-making processes. It follows that re-designing jobs in order to remove the causes of overloading – particularly overloading due to the pace of the job, or speed stress – would enable older workers to cope much more successfully with skilled work.

As a person becomes older we can assume that his store of knowledge becomes larger. This increase in knowledge may help to overcome some of the short-term storage and decision-speed problems associated with age: a worker who has been in a particular job for many years will have accumulated a store of 'tricks of the trade' which a younger worker may not have developed, and which may offset the loss in performance caused by the slowing of decision-making ability. However, too much knowledge may produce problems of its own: an older worker may have many more responses to choose from than a younger worker, and therefore may be slower at retrieving information from memory storage and making decisions. This situation might occur especially in those skilled jobs which require a high degree of flexibility of response. Also it is sometimes found that older workers are less flexible in their ideas and attitudes; this may be the result of their greater experience. While this may be useful in determining the best course of action to follow it may also lead to prejudices against the best decisions and methods: 'We can't try this new technique, we've always done it the old way.'

If we accept Welford's belief that older workers are working nearer their full capacity, at least in some of the skills they use, it is also probable that any environmental strain imposed on them will more readily have adverse effects than it will on younger workers. Temperature and humidity, noise, light and glare may therefore have more marked effects on an older worker's performance. Research suggests that high temperature and humidity result in more accidents among older workers than among the young; glare, too, often has a greater effect on older workers.

'The Older, the Wiser'

The evidence described so far produces a rather disheartening view of the effects of ageing on performance. The adage 'You can't teach an old dog new tricks' can be interpreted to mean that older people are incapable of learning anything new. Some theorists go even further and maintain that in addition the individual's IQ declines fairly rapidly with age.

However, some areas of research demonstrate that all is not so gloomy as was originally supposed. First, ageing may not lead to a drastic physical decline. Secondly, through the use of well designed training systems older workers can learn new jobs very well indeed – in some cases, better than younger workers. Thirdly, it appears that the decline in IQ with age is not so marked as was at first thought, and in some respects IQ scores continue to improve throughout life.

Little Physical Decline

It has been assumed that a drastic physical decline accompanies ageing, but when careful measurements of such changes are made, some rather surprising results emerge; for example, compared with a person aged 20, an 80-year-old loses on average only 15 to 20 per cent brain weight; in speed of neural conduction he loses only 15 to 20 per cent; and he loses only 25 per cent of muscle strength.

New Training Systems

Some of the most influential work on training of older workers has been carried out by E. and R.M. Belbin. When older workers are compared with twenty- to forty-year-olds it is frequently found that they learn new tasks considerably less well. The Belbins believed that this might not be because of a total inability to learn, but because of the older workers' inability to learn by the methods used for younger workers. If a training programme were to be devised using learning techniques which reduced the need for holding information in short-term memory storage – which, as we have seen, older people have some difficulty in doing – they might be able to improve their learning abilities.

The Belbins decided that three aspects of conventional learning methods posed problems for older workers:

1 Having to translate a series of verbal instructions into actions; for example, translating 'You turn the left handle, then push the red button and at the same time pull the big lever down' into actions was difficult because it involved memorizing a sequence of controls and actions.

2 Understanding instructions, particularly if they were new, long and complicated.

3 'Unlearning' incorrect work habits or wrong procedures once they had been learnt.

One of their experiments, carried out at a wool mill, concerned the training of workers employed to mend miswoven fabric. The traditional method of training was for a new trainee to sit next to an experienced mender, who performed the job and explained to the trainee what to do. The Belbins' approach was different. Instead of being given complicated verbal instructions, the older trainees were encouraged to do the work. First they were allowed to practise mending weaves with larger-scale weaves, specially made of thick elastic so that errors in the weave could be easily seen and were quite easy to mend. Next, the trainees began to mend actual thread weaves but could view their work through magnifying lenses, so that they had a clearer view of what they were doing. By showing the trainees what was required visually, instead of verbally, the important parts of the task could be emphasized without causing confusion.

The results were quite startling. The older workers were given eight hours of guided instruction and practice on the enlarged weaves, then twelve hours' solo practice – a total of twenty hours. The time taken to mend different types of weave was compared with the time taken by groups of fifteen-year-old school-leavers, some of whom had been given the new training method, and some the traditional. After twenty hours' experience older workers could mend most types of weaves in approximately three to five minutes. It took most of the fifteen-year-olds between three and ten weeks to reach the same standard, even when using the new training method. Thus the new training method benefited the older workers much more than the fifteen-year-olds; the findings provide strong support for the belief that removing the necessity for memorizing helps older workers to learn.

The Belbins pointed out, however, that some older workers may be quite able to memorize. Like any skill, they argue, the ability to memorize may be lost through lack of use; if an individual continues to exercise the ability throughout life, little deterioration should occur. But for those workers who do have difficulty in memorizing, techniques like the Belbins' can be extremely helpful.

Does Intelligence Decline with Age?
This issue is complicated by two factors. First, as we have already seen, there is no universally accepted definition of 'intelligence', so

that the above question should really read, 'Does IQ decline with age?' The second problem is that even when we try to answer this question the findings are not conclusive. This is because adult IQ has until recently been studied using the cross-sectional method. The same IQ test is given to a group of twenty-year-olds, a group of thirty-year-olds, and so on, up to a group of subjects aged eighty to ninety. With this kind of research it appears that IQ does decline with age, and particularly those abilities which require the use of short-term memory; other abilities, such as vocabulary and general knowledge, appear to be little affected. However, the problem is that it is unlikely that the only difference between, for example, a group of twenty-year-olds and a group of eighty-year-olds will be age. The eighty-year-olds will have lived through different experiences such as wars, and perhaps poverty; they will almost certainly have had less formal education than current twenty-year-olds. It could be that the cause of the measured decline in IQ is these different experiences, rather than simple ageing.

More recently an alternative method of investigation has become more widely used to study any decline of IQ with age. This is known as the longitudinal method (on page 149 the same method was used for child studies); it involves giving IQ tests to the same individuals at regular intervals throughout life. Because we are thus comparing the same individual at different ages, any decline in IQ should be caused by ageing. Obviously such studies take a long time to complete, but early results suggest that there is remarkably little decline in IQ with age, although it could be argued that experience of several IQ tests throughout life may give falsely inflated IQ scores because the individual has in effect been able to practise. Vocabulary and general-knowledge abilities do not seem to be affected much by age, and in fact often continue to increase throughout life.

Mark Rosenzweig performed experiments with rats which – if it is possible to apply rat results to humans – offer hope of preventing decline with age. Rats which are reared in stimulating environments with plenty of toys and objects to manipulate remain more 'intelligent' throughout life, and show much less decline in ability with age.

The Years of Retirement

For the individual who is about to retire, three general attitudes to his new situation seem possible: he may be delighted because he now has the time to do all those things he has never had time to concentrate on before; he may feel neutral, believing that it will not really make much difference to him; or he may be frightened that he has been in a sense rejected by society, is no longer wanted, and has nothing to look forward to. But is there one common attitude among people who are about to retire or have already retired?

In their book *Growing Old* (Basic Books, 1961) M.E. Cumming and W.E. Henry suggested that most people, irrespective of their attitudes to retirement, would in practice feel fearful and rejected when it actually occurred. They proposed that when a person retires from work he begins to disengage himself from society. Their ideas form the basis of 'social disengagement theory'. Most people in our culture retire at the age of sixty to sixty-five years. Usually their lives have revolved round their work and the friends and contacts at work, but on retirement these social bonds are more difficult to maintain because the friends are generally still at work while the retired individual is at home. In addition the older person's capacities decline, both physically and psychologically; he cannot use his dwindling energies in travelling to visit friends, who are often more fully occupied anyway and may not have time to see him, so that their numbers are likely to decrease. Consequently, according to the theory, the disengaging individual psychologically 'pulls in his horns' and begins to withdraw from social contacts and activities. He also becomes less emotionally attached to and involved with other people. This increased isolation from society may be, theorists believe, some kind of preparation – possibly innate – for death. This theory of disengagement therefore implies that the process is the result of two factors – an external economic force which requires people to retire from their roles as earners in the economic system at a certain age, and an internal, developmental process by which the individual adapts to live with and accept his reducing energies.

If this interpretation is correct the outlook seems a depressing one. Now that life expectancy is greater, individuals will have more time between retirement and death, most of which will be spent in greater or lesser disengagement from society. Is this inevitable? Does everyone go through this process, or might the individual be able to adapt himself to changed circumstances in other ways? Many people develop wider interests, both intellectual and social, when they have retired, while others refuse to retire at all. Thus social disengagement theory does not apply equally to everybody. Individuals previously employed in research or intellectual work will be able to continue with it, while those who have worked on production lines will not be able to maintain an equivalent interest. Those giving up highly regarded jobs may feel deeply the sudden loss of prestige, but individuals who have worked in low-status jobs will not feel the loss so much. Women who have not gone out to work may not undergo the change of retirement at all, nor will they disengage because friends and relations will still be around them; on the other hand some may suffer the effects of a husband's disengagement if he is constantly 'under their feet'. Even among people who have retired from similar jobs there will be individual differences in the extent of their social disengagement, just as people who have not retired differ in their need for social contacts. The range of people's interests before retirement, and even their spending power, will affect their ability to cope with and enjoy the change in their life. With so large a number of factors playing a part, individuals will not want to, or be able to, disengage to the same extent.

Also, while there may be a change in the quantity of social contacts, these may improve in quality. The number of friends may be fewer, but relationships with remaining friends can become closer and more personal, perhaps simply because there is more time for this to happen after retirement. Such an increase in the intensity of personal contacts may compensate for their smaller number, a point which the disengagement theorists often do not realize.

Disengagement therefore does occur in some individuals, but it would be a mistake to regard it as the course of nature or the inevitable result of ageing. Several external factors associated with ageing – lack of mobility, lack of money, or an inability to continue work – are more likely to lead to disengagement than any psychological tendencies. Once these factors have been isolated, preventative measures can be taken to reduce the chances of disengagement for those individuals who prefer to maintain a full interaction with others and with society. There is danger in a society's complete acceptance of disengagement as a natural or inevitable process: the theory leads us to believe that old people should be withdrawn from society and perhaps put in homes or institutions, even when they would prefer to play, and are capable of fulfilling, their full social and economic roles. An ability which is not used may atrophy; perhaps we ought to be providing more opportunities for individuals to practise their skills, abilities and interests well before retirement age – through pre-retirement courses, for example – so that on retirement they will have at their disposal a series of skills and interests which will allow them to remain active and involved in society. For those who become socially disengaged against their will, social-work agencies and voluntary groups are now attempting to provide visitors and helpers for the isolated elderly. Government-sponsored television advertisements have recently been shown, encouraging people to take an interest in the isolated elderly around them. While this interest is mainly concerned with preventing illness, or even death through cold in winter, it is also a useful step towards ensuring psychological well-being, because a regular visitor may encourage the isolated individual to interact more and provide links with potential friends.

When a lifetime friend or spouse moves away or dies, the individual is said to be *desolated*: there is nobody left in whom to confide, or with whom to have a deep emotional relationship. It is often desolation which produces the deepest feelings of loneliness, stronger even than those experienced in isolation. The desolated individual may have other friends and acquaintances who are willing to help but because of the loss of the deep emotional relationship will still feel lonely. In cases of bereavement the family can often provide support; sometimes, however, this gradually fades away after a few weeks or months, and the desolated person is left to cope with life alone – possibly for the first time in many years.

In the past many old people who showed disturbed behaviour – gross disturbances of attention, memory and thinking, withdrawal from reality, and hallucinations – were assumed to be suffering irreversible deterioration of the brain; this organic decay was known as *senile dementia*. However, post-mortem examinations of the brains of such people showed that although some were suffering from fairly wide-scale brain deterioration many showed no obvious organic cause for their inappropriate behaviour. Psychiatrists are now adopting the view that in many such cases the cause is depression. This means that they can often be improved by the careful use of anti-depressant drugs. Because depression, unlike organic brain decay, is often assumed to have an environmental cause, steps can be taken to prevent it by helping the individual to adjust to new patterns of life and providing care, attention, affection and stimulation. It should however be noted that in the long term large doses of anti-depressant and sleep-producing drugs may cause a patient to seem confused. It has recently been shown that some old people who were thought to be suffering from depression-produced dementia were in fact suffering from the amount of drugs used to combat their condition. When the drug doses were stopped or reduced the effects largely disappeared.

Much more research is needed into the effects of retirement, disengagement and ageing generally. The assumption has been that an individual always declines with age, but it has become obvious that not all individuals do so; in fact many manage to make rapid and efficient adaptations to their changed environments. Perhaps the research effort might more profitably be directed towards investigating how these successful adaptations are achieved, rather than why they do not occur in some people.

The End of Life

Psychologists are unable as yet to formulate laws of human behaviour which will always apply. However, one event in life is predictable, and that is that at some point life will end. Yet in spite of its inevitability – and perhaps because of it – death and the period leading up to it, the *terminal phase*, are very much ignored. Often people regard the terminal phase and death as the worst part of life, the part that involves unpleasantness and wastage, to be endured when it actually happens but not to be discussed beforehand. Most people have witnessed unpleasant scenes of death first- or second-hand and so the belief has developed that death is always painful, messy, frightening and a thing to be shut out of mind. However, today we have the medical technology to prolong life and to make dying less painful physically.

But what of the psychological effects of death on both the dying individual and relations and friends? We shall consider some of the factors which affect the emotional adaptation of the individual, and those whom he leaves, when death occurs in old age or at the end of a terminal illness. First, there is a tendency for relatives and friends to deny that death is near, but not telling him about approaching death may lead to uncertainty and anxiety: if he knows that death is coming he can prepare himself for it. Secondly, death can be the final stage of human development. The individual has the chance to assess his life, and perhaps to put right any wrongs he has done to others. Legal aspects such as the writing or altering of a will may need to be attended to, along with the emotional aspect of comforting and reassuring friends and relatives. For some people religion assumes an important role, both in reducing anxiety for the dying person and in providing comfort for relatives.

Finally, as we have mentioned, with modern medical care, pain, even in agonizing terminal illnesses, can be much reduced. Hospitals deal quickly and well with incontinence or bleeding, so that physical care of the dying is often satisfactory. However, most hospitals are impersonal places and it may be better – particularly when no intensive physical treatment is required – to allow the patient to go home to die, so that he is in familiar surroundings and can have friends and relatives present if desired.

Throughout life, the individual develops methods of adapting himself to his environment, and vice versa. The approach of death is the last opportunity for him to do so, and many people succeed in this, the final adaptation. It is the job of psychologists to provide advice and understanding of this area and, as research develops, we can hope that the traditional picture of dying will disappear, to be replaced by a new approach. The new view, which has inspired this book, would emphasize the importance of the individual's ability to predict, meet and solve the problems posed by his environment; this ability enables him to live a happy and useful life with a peaceful end.

Summary

1 Ageing is commonly supposed to lead to physical and intellectual decline, but recent research indicates that this need not always be the case.
2 Although short-term memory and decision speed decline in the elderly, lack of practice rather than ageing may be a major cause of these changes and appropriate training techniques may combat them.
3 Intelligence is also supposed to decline with age, but this finding may be the result of the cross-sectional study method used in investigating IQ changes. An elderly person may have a lower measured IQ than a younger person because he has had different experiences, not because he is older. Lifelong studies of the changes in individuals' IQs with age suggest that IQ may not decline greatly over the years, and that some aspects of intelligent behaviour may improve with ageing.

4 Disengagement theory proposes that individuals who retire tend to cut their social contacts and begin to withdraw from life – partly by choice, and partly because of economic pressure. However, there appear to be such large individual differences in the extent of disengagement that it is not possible to believe that the process is a natural one, or inevitable on retirement.

5 With the loss of contacts with friends and relatives an individual may become isolated; the death of or separation from a spouse or particular friend can sever deep affection bonds; the individual may be desolated, suffering from intense depression and loneliness. This can lead to symptoms similar to those caused by organic brain decay; however, depression, unlike organic decay, may be alleviated.

6 Death is an unpleasant subject in our culture; we pretend death is not there, and are more shocked and frightened than necessary when it does occur. Modern medicine has improved the physical care of the terminal patient, but at the same time individuals and their friends and relatives need to accept the fact of death and to prepare for it. The task of psychologists is, through research, to help people to adapt to these circumstances, as they adapt to changing patterns of events throughout life.

List of Further Reading

Topics

Argyle, M., *The Psychology of Inter-personal Behaviour* (Penguin, 1967).
— Non-verbal communication, self-concept

Argyle, M., *The Social Psychology of Work* (Penguin, 1974).
— Work

Borger, R. and Seaborne, A.E.M., *The Psychology of Learning* (Penguin, 1967).
— Learning

Bromley, D.B., *The Psychology of Human Aging* (Penguin, 1965).
— Ageing

Brown, R., *Social Psychology* (Collier Macmillan, 1965).
— Piaget, Bruner, conformity

Carter, C.O., *Human Heredity*, 2nd ed (Penguin, 1977).
— Genetics, physiology

Gregory, R.L., *Eye and Brain: the Psychology of Seeing*, 3rd ed. (Weidenfeld & Nicolson, 1977).
— Perception, including physiology

Greene, J., *Thinking and Language* (Methuen, 1975).
— Piaget, Bruner

Manning, A., *An Introduction to Animal Behaviour*, 2nd ed. (Edward Arnold, 1972).
— Learning, Critical or Sensitive Periods, physiology, genetics Maternal deprivation

Rutter, M. *Maternal Deprivation Reassessed* (Penguin, 1972).

Index

movement, visual perception, 35–6
Muller–Lyer illusion, 61–2
Mundugumor, 150–1
'muscle memory', 101
muscles, nervous system, 5, 10, 22
Mussen, P., 167
mutation, genetic, 50
myelin sheath, 2, 10, 16

nativists, 53, 60, 61, 124
nature/nurture debate: intelligence, 65,
111–23; visual perception, 52–66; *see
also* environment, genetics
Nazis, 181
negative reinforcement, 84–5, 144, 196
negroes, intelligence, 118–19
neonates, *see* babies
nerve cells, *see* neurons
nerve gases, 7
nerves, 9, 24
nervous system: interaction with endocrine system, 25; physiology, 1–24
neurons: biofeedback, 88; Classical
Conditioning, 76; cortical, 16; learning processes, 68–70; neural conduction, 5–7, 112, 113, 207; physiology, 1–7, 9, 16, 40; random firing, 205
New Guinea, 150–1
Newman, H.H., 116, 118
Newson, J. and E., 153–4, 160
night-shift workers, 191
noise, influence on behaviour, 187–8,
206
non-verbal communication (NVC), 169–
75
noradrenalin, 26, 191
norms, work, 199
Nottingham, study of aggression, 153–4
nurture/nature debate, *see* nature/
nurture debate

occipital lobe, brain, 21
oestrogen, 27
Olds, J., 87
open field test, 48–9
Operant Conditioning, 60, 77–94, 141,
144–6
ossicles, 39

outer ear, 37–8
oval window, inner ear, 39

pain, and maternal deprivation, 133
parasympathetic nervous system, 10, 11,
12
parents: child-rearing styles, 148–61;
and child's sex-role identification, 141,
144–6, 150–1; development of child's
self-concept, 164
parietal lobe, brain, 21–2
Paris, Education Department, 110
pattern, babies' perception of, 59
Patton, R.G., 134
Pavlov, I., 71–2, 74, 77
Pavlovian Conditioning, 71–2
perception: in animals, 73; brain's control of, 20; nature/nurture debate, 52–
66; visual, 29–37, 56–7, 61–3
perceptual constancy, 59–60, 61–3
peripheral nervous system, 9–16, 17
permissive parents, 154, 156–7
Pfungst, A., 174–5
phase sequences, 70, 95, 97, 112
phenotype, 43
phenylalanine, 47
phenylketonuria (PKU), 47–8, 119
phobias, 74–6
phylogenesis, 65
physical punishment, 149–50, 151–3,
154
physiological psychology, 1–27
Piaget, J., 95–9, 100–1, 106, 111, 124,
162, 184
pigeons, reinforced behaviour, 81, 82–
3
pinna, 38
pitch, sound-waves, 37, 39
pituitary gland, 25, 26–7
pleasure centre, hypothalamus, 87
polygenic characteristics, 48–9
positive reinforcement, 84, 144, 196
posture, non-verbal communication, 169
pre-operational stage, child development, 96, 99, 124
privation, 136
problem solving, 91–3
programmed learning, 88–9